POSITIVE PRAISE:

"With the ever-increasing pressures on our young people to perform well in their education, the rise in mental ill-health and the information overload society is learning to manage, Lesley has written a book that will not only help parents help their kids in their growth and development, but all adults willing to read and undertake the exercises shared. This easy to read guide inspires you to consider where you are right now and tune in to what you really want. When we go for what we want it ignites a spark of passion which is the fuel of living a happy fulfilled life with no limits on our dreams. Don't you want that for your kids? This book will get you and them on the right track."

Becky Hill
– Founder/CEO, Solutions 42 Ltd

Lesley Strachan has synthesized her 30+ years of coaching, educational research and experience to provide a wonderful guide for the seekers of living a purposeful life. Lesley's deep knowledge within this area allows both students and adults alike to learn what it takes to create a masterful life for oneself. Full of enlightening stories and excellent but gentle exercises, this book is a must-have to learn more about finding one's path.

Rod Ezekiel
– Chief Inspiration Officer, Souls Quest

Copyright © 2018 by Lesley Strachan

Published in the United Kingdom by Librotas Books
Portsmouth, Hampshire
PO2 9NT
www.librotas.com

ISBN (Print): 978-1-9996315-2-9
ISBN (eBook): 978-1-9996315-3-6

All rights reserved. No part of this book may be reproduced or transmitted in any form or by any means, electronic or mechanical, including photocopying, recording or by any information storage and retrieval system, without written permission from the author, except for the inclusion of brief quotations in a review.

Jack J. Lesyk has granted the Author permission to utilise his Nine Mental Skills of Successful Athletes.

Limit of Liability Disclaimer: The information contained in this book is for information purposes only and may not apply to your situation. The author, publisher, distributor and provider provide no warranty about the content or accuracy of content enclosed. Information provided is subjective. Keep this in mind when reviewing this guide.

Neither the publisher nor author shall be liable for any loss of profit or any other commercial damages resulting from use of this guide. All links are for information purposes only and are not warranted for content, accuracy, or any other implied or explicit purpose.

Earnings Disclaimer: All income examples in this book are just that – examples. They are not intended to represent or guarantee that everyone will achieve the same results. You understand that everyone's success will be determined by his or her desire, dedication, background, effort and motivation to work. There is no guarantee you will duplicate any of the results stated here. You recognize any business endeavour has inherent risk for loss of capital.

The typical result one can expect to achieve is nothing. The 'typical' person never gets to the end of this book. The 'typical' person fails to implement anything. Thus, they earn nothing. Zero. No income. And perhaps a loss of income. That's because 'typical' people do nothing and therefore they achieve nothing. Be atypical. Do something. Implement something. If it doesn't work, make a change… and implement that. Try again… try harder. Persist. And reap the rewards.

THE ULTIMATE GUIDE FOR PARENTS

How to help your kids become self-confident, happy and passionate

LESLEY STRACHAN

Table of Contents

Introduction   7

Chapter 1   17
Responsibility: How to Help Young People to Take Responsibility for Their Life

Chapter 2   25
Grades – Who Cares? How to Find Out What You Love to Do

Chapter 3   37
What Do You Want from Life?

Chapter 4   47
Let's Find Out What You Love to Do

Chapter 5   53
Let's Get to the Point: Clarifying Your Vision of Your Ideal Life

Chapter 6   73
Out with the Old: How to Believe Your Vision Is Possible

Chapter 7   91
Life Overload: How to Make It Through the Day with a Coach

Chapter 8   105
Reflecting on Where You Are Now

Chapter 9   115
Follow-up Framework

Chapter 10   117
Where Do I Go from Here?

Chapter 11   119
How to Get Help

BIBLIOGRAPHY   121

ABOUT THE AUTHOR   123

Quantity Discounts   127

BONUS!   129

Introduction

"The future depends on what you do today."
Mahatma Gandhi

"Everyone needs a coach" – some of the most successful people in the world have a coach including Bill Gates, Eric Schmidt and Tony Robbins. Coaching is an excellent technique for both adults and young people to gain a different perspective on life and to get feedback on what they're doing. I agree and strongly believe that whether the coaching is professional or voluntary, it needs to be more closely in tune with the needs and aspirations of those being coached to be effective, because we're all different.

Thinking back to our school days, we were taught various subjects, given a bit of guidance about what career we should follow and that's about it. There weren't, and still aren't, any excellent coaching programmes in schools unless you're an athlete. Furthermore, with recent UK government policy suggesting that all young people should have a coach or mentor, it's difficult to see how this would work in practical terms. This situation continues to be of concern since the education sector continues to cut budgets and careers services, which I'm going to talk about in greater detail later.

During my teaching career I've never seen or experienced how schools, colleges and universities and, for that matter, workplaces tap into the root passions that we are all born with. Imagine if the education system tapped into our core passions and promoted educational subjects around those passions instead of trying to pigeonhole everyone?

As we get older it doesn't get much better. How many adults do you know that are stuck in a job they have no passion for? It might even be you! Employers who have training budgets train them in the skills and capabilities to do the job. What they don't do enough of is align people's passions, skills and abilities to the organization's purpose. Wouldn't the country be more productive if we all loved our lives and our jobs? Maybe it's something we should all aspire to?

Having worked with thousands of young people, my purpose in life is to inspire and support parents, guardians and those who meet young people to coach them towards a life and career filled with purpose and have fun doing it. That is the reason why I've written this book.

I love what I do because of the results I get working with both adults and young people. I see people's eyes light up when they realize what's possible and they see a future for themselves. This is particularly important for what we describe as the lost generation of children. With adults I experience people ditching the jobs they hate and starting to follow their true passion in life. With young people I love to see them discover what they want to do in life as this helps them focus on their choice of studies. What's your story going to be?

This is not a book of good ideas. This is a book of timeless principles used by successful people all over the world. I have studied these Success Principles for over 10 years and have applied them to my own life. My success includes being an award-winning coach, consultant, trainer, speaker and adviser to thousands of young people and adults in the UK, Europe, USA and South Africa. I get to travel which I love to do and network with positive like-minded professionals daily.

Who this book is for

When I first started writing this book I thought that parents would be the obvious people to coach their own young people through this workbook, and they very well might be. I hope you are one of the fortunate parents who know exactly what they want from life.

However, sometimes parents themselves do not have a clear idea about what they want either, so it may be hard to coach their kids. If you aren't clear about what you want from life, then I would highly recommend that you work through this book yourself before coaching your kids through the process.

In an ideal world my aim is for parents, carers and young people to work together through the book simultaneously doing the exercises together so that both of you learn, develop and grow. It's a great opportunity to also find out more about each other and what makes you both tick. The same applies to carers, career advisers and anyone else involved with advising young people.

Some of the feedback I had in the early drafts of this book suggested that parents could hand this book to their young people to read. Yet in my experience reading a book is generally one of the last things children born into a digital age want to do. Which is why I've designed some micro webinars so that they can watch them instead via our website http://bit.ly/Free4Members and then do the exercises. That said, in my experience of working with young adults aged 14-18, they achieve better progress if they are guided through it.

If you have older children (18+) it's possible they would like to work through this book on their own with some support from you. Whatever works for you, works for me. Alternatively, you may want your kids to work with me as their coach and I can do that for young people aged 14-21 and work with you as their parent as well for maximum impact.

You may also be attracted to the book if you're involved with young people as careers advisers in schools, colleges and universities. You can learn how to coach and mentor young people using techniques that really work and make a significant difference in addition to the careers advice support on offer. What is helpful is for careers advisers to help young people work through these exercises before offering careers advice so that young people have the self-confidence and are happy and passionate about the choices they then make about their future.

Why have I written this book?

I've written this book because success hasn't come easy for me. I was adopted at six weeks old into a working-class family who worked hard and gave me a strong, stable base in a loving relationship. My dad worked a full-time job and worked extra hours at the weekend to make ends meet. My mum was a stay-at-home mum who devoted herself to my brother and me. When Dad came home she went and worked part time to bring some extra cash into the household. I think that's where I get my work ethic from.

As a child I was encouraged to try all types of activities and spent all my formative years at a dancing school studying classical ballet, tap, modern and national dancing. I took exams and had leading roles in our annual pantomimes over the years. Mum made my costumes and paid for all my tuition and my dad took the role of taxi driver and acted as my ballet barre for years whilst I practised my art. My passion for dance gave me my early successes through passing exams. It built my confidence because I was shy, and you can't be shy whilst on stage performing. Performing also enabled me to act and play many different characters which I still use on occasion in life when I feel overawed in certain situations. Dance also taught me self-discipline and commitment and an ability to follow my passion.

The interesting thing is that although I accumulated all these skills and abilities all I wanted later in my teenage years was to be a hippy! Perhaps I was inwardly rebelling and the thought of wandering on a beach barefoot with long hair and flowers in my hair was quite appealing… well, maybe that will happen one day!

At the start of my secondary education the whole family emigrated to Australia. Here I finished school with the equivalent of three GCSEs because dancing was my passion and I spent every waking moment in dance class instead of studying. I started work at 16 in the Bank of New South Wales so that I could make money, although I would have preferred to dance for a living. I didn't go to college or university because I didn't want to. However, I did go back to 'school' to complete an MBA later in life. I also worked hard to get a series of professional qualifications.

I got married and gave up my full-time job and opened a dance and drama school which fulfilled me because I was earning a living and following my passions again. A divorce meant that I ended up living on benefits of £34 a week, so I know what it's like to scrape the bottom of the barrel whilst bringing up a three-year-old on your own. I made the decision to wind up the dance and drama school and go back into a full-time job in marketing to pay the mortgage and pay off my debts. I brought up my son alone for 10 years before marrying for the second time, to my wonderful husband who is super supportive.

Throughout my career whether working part time or full time, I'd never had a coach or mentor. Until 2008. Instead I educated myself through lifelong learning courses to get better qualifications. This aspect of continual learning never stops because you and I will always have some days that are better than others. Sometimes it's even a struggle to get from one day to the next.

How do I know that? Because occasionally it also happens to me as well. What gets me through the difficult days now is the mindset I have been able to embrace through all I've learnt using the Success Principles by Jack Canfield.

In 2008, during one of the more difficult parts of my life, I enrolled on the Success Principles programme. This was the first time in my life that I had had a coach to inspire and support me. The results I achieved throughout the programme were phenomenal. I became passionate about wanting to inspire and support other people to achieve the kinds of changes they want to make in their lives whether these are large or small. Since I knew the principles and techniques worked I decided to become a Certified Trainer in the Success Principles and graduated in 2015.

Since then I have taught these principles and techniques to thousands of people. Recently I worked with a group of postgraduate students in a module called Personal & Professional Development. Because of them applying the Success Principles many of these students have gone on to pursue passions in their lives and careers that they didn't even know they had until they did the programme.

I was so impressed with one group that I held a party called 'Come as you are in 2026' and filmed the event. During this role-playing exercise one film student came up to me and introduced himself as the successor to David Attenborough – the BBC wildlife expert and broadcaster. He told me that his plan was to work for the BBC and follow in the footsteps of this iconic broadcaster. He graphically described his life, and where he lived (obviously pretending at this point) and talked about the places where he had travelled and filmed for the BBC, and he was alight with passion and enthusiasm. Watch his and other students' stories here http://bit.ly/YouTubeLesley.

Wouldn't you like a similar situation for yourself or the young people in your life? Well you can, because you've already taken the first step by getting hold of this book. The book is rooted in the Success Principles methodology and filled with simple exercises to complete, inspirational quotes and real stories from real people. I hope these will inspire and motivate you to act and make the changes you want to make.

It's important to say right now that whilst life is fluid and unpredictable, these are tried and tested principles that will never change. In fact, they will only increase in effectiveness as you use them daily.

I'm not just saying that – I am living proof that they work, and thousands of other people all over the world are learning how to develop their passions to create the life they want to live. The phenomenal level of success that I now enjoy is the result of not just knowing the principles and techniques but consistently applying them day in and day out.

As R. Buckminster Fuller, who was a designer, inventor and futurist once said:

> *"If you want to teach people a new way of thinking, don't bother trying to teach them. Instead, give them a tool, the use of which will lead to a new way of thinking."*

Therefore, what you'll find in this book are the stable principles and tools to help you think and act differently if you choose to do so. In other words, they work… when you implement them. They don't work if you just read about them without taking any action. They are based on the rock-solid strategies that we have been using with adults and young people for years.

You can view and read the latest success stories of other people who've been through this programme on our website. We're also always adding new stories, testimonials and free resources which can found here https://lesley-strachan-consulting-training.com/. One piece of advice: use the resources. They will help you get more out of the principles and practices in this book.

On that note, the difference between average people and great people comes down to implementation. I know I've said this already but it's true; knowing what to do isn't the same as doing it and seeing the positive results you'll get.

When this information is implemented it can make a profound difference to your life and the lives of the young people in your life. One person often differs from another only in their willingness to implement the things they learn. Are you ready to get working with me? Use the tools and techniques in this book and then send your success story to lesley@lesleystrachan.co.uk.

However, not everyone knows what they want. I didn't at one point in my life. One of the most common statements I get from both adults and young people is, "How am I supposed to know what I want to do with my life or choose the right career?"

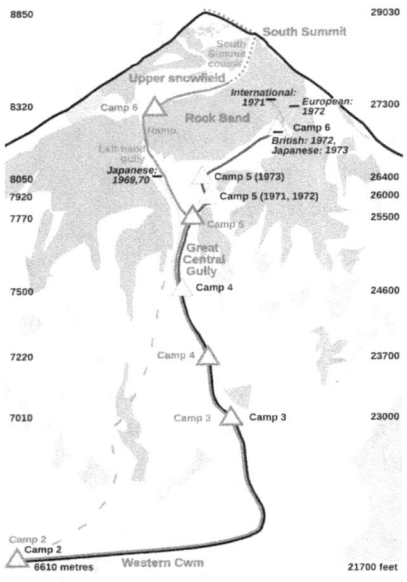

Mount Everest, climbing routes of Southwest Face

For those who do know what they want, life is not always easy and straightforward. To use a simple analogy, some people dream of being on an expedition to climb Mount Everest (or its equivalent in their life). Those who join the expedition create a plan and have a passion for the journey. They head towards the summit.

Along the way (as in life), they aim for a series of base camps which mark points where people acclimatize themselves and prepare for the next stage in the journey. The whole journey is broken down into short, manageable targets, and then further broken down into specific actionable steps which may even be daily targets. Then it's a matter of focusing on the plan and making adjustments, large or small, along the way until you reach the summit. The same applies to you at this stage of your journey.

However, whilst some people know what they want and have a passion, other people aren't yet aware. That's OK because starting at base camp is a great place to start.

That's the purpose of this book – to give you inspiration and support to plan your own personal journey, and for your young people to do the same. The inspiration will come from me, and from you, and other supportive people you may want to help you. On that note, towards the end of the book, I have included a section on where and how to find people to help you implement the strategies in this book.

Before I got started writing this book I wanted to find out what parents and guardians worried about the most as they brought up their young people.

So, I asked over 2,000 people who look after young people, "What are the three things that worry you about your child's future?" The responses fell into several categories:

Finance – Financial independence, financial self-sufficiency, to be prosperous and be able to choose what to do.

Job or career – To know what job or career path to follow.

Free time – Rediscover the things we did in our free time but have stopped because of other pressures on our time.

Physical health – Eating healthily, drug addiction, tackling obesity, getting my kids to eat vegetables.

Relationships – Wisdom in their relationships, marrying poorly, not being a good enough parent.

Personal life – Self-confidence, to be happy amongst the chaos in the world, to improve low self-esteem and belief in themselves. To be passionate about what they do, to be happy, self-reliant, loving, mindful and worldly. To be able to fail and learn from the mistakes made. To stop being fearful and lazy.

Community – Climate change, increasing inequality, global corporate dominance, loss of public services, education system, war, education funding, social media pressures.

This word cloud was generated using the concerns that adults have for the future of their young people. Can you see anything that applies to your young people or you?

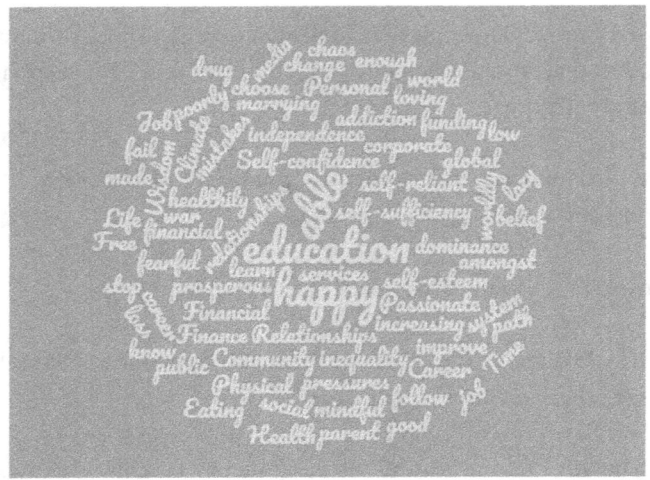

The good news is that I am going to cover these areas in the exercises throughout this book. However, you can pick and choose and focus on one specific area that's on your mind right now and sort that area out first. The choice is yours, so let's get started!

CHAPTER 1

Responsibility: How to Help Young People to Take Responsibility for Their Life

---

Congratulations! Just by getting to this first chapter, you're already way ahead of your friends and family. Why? Well, most people don't take the necessary action for success. You've got this far; now let's go the rest of the way together. At least you're forward thinking. You know that getting young people to take responsibility for their own lives is a big deal, and you think that they are probably bobbing along very well, and you might use the careers services on offer to drum up some enthusiasm from them, or to give them some inspiration, if that service is still available to you.

You may think that the information from the internet, school, college, or university will help you, or it may in fact be confusing. There's so much information out there and you're going to get a lot of facts and figures about this career and that option. Who searches for a coach who will help the young people get from where they are now to where they want to be – or discover where they want to be? Not many people, I suspect.

The status of careers support/advice

Recent research by Dr. Deirdre Hughes OBE[1] shows that, increasingly, the current careers support system in England is broken, with too much reliance on informality and hard-to-navigate information. There has been a serious de-professionalization of careers work in England's schools, with young people and families missing out on vital information and support. Whilst there is endless information available online, in the end people like human interaction and prefer a personal connection.

Having inspirational activities for young people in schools and colleges with exposure to employers and mentors is a good thing. Organizations such as Young Enterprise, Business in the Community, the National Careers Service, Careers and Enterprise Company, Job Centre Plus, education business partnerships and national charities are all working to this similar end, which is excellent.

Mentoring young people is high on the government's agenda but is still in its infancy and not available to everyone and isn't very well funded, with the majority of mentors volunteering their time to schools. I mentor in a secondary school in Southampton and there are only six students in the whole school who have access to the mentoring programme because these are the students that the school feels would benefit the most. Furthermore, informal encounters and random acts of kindness from employers, mentors and volunteers alone will not solve much-needed careers support for Britain's young people. This approach is only part of the solution.

For the last five years, schools have had to fund careers guidance from their overall budget as the £200 million dedicated budget was withdrawn from local authorities. For many, this has proved extremely challenging, and further cuts are on the horizon. The National Audit Office indicates that schools in England must reduce spending by 8% per pupil by 2020, and it is likely that careers guidance is in danger of dropping even further down the list of priorities.

With the move towards young people having a portfolio career and 'the gig economy' becoming increasingly popular, more people will need to trade on their skills and experiences. Working in a gig economy means that instead of earning a regular wage, workers get paid for the 'gigs' they do, such as a food delivery or a car journey... Meanwhile, workers in the gig economy are classed as independent contractors. This is very different from the type of employment you as parents are used to. Your kids will probably not stay in the same job for life, and they need transferable skills to stay employed in whatever job or sector they go into.

To achieve awareness on this scale, it is vital that young people with your inspiration and support become aware of who they are, and what they want to be, so that they can contribute towards economic growth in their communities.

It makes sense when you think about it. You can even look to your own life as proof of this changing world; how often do you see people staying in the same job for their lifetime anymore? Do you worry about your kid's future and job prospects? How aware are you of what your kid's passions and skills are? Are you currently coaching them towards being the successful individuals they want to be – not what you want them to be?

What is surprising to me, as a life and career coach, is the vast number of young people I've taught who go to college and university with no idea at all as to why they are there. Every year without fail thousands of students graduate and end up working in jobs they are not sure about or, worse still, no job at all along with debts they cannot repay. This isn't a passing trend and is here to stay for the foreseeable future with over 50% of the students being very unsure of what they want from life.

Career guidance is great but does not provide the holistic experience that coaching offers. Coaching is a lifelong learning opportunity for the young people in your life, and for you as a responsible adult. The tools and techniques that I use ensure that they are inspired and motivated towards a life and career they will be engaged with and make progress in (if they work with the principles).

What that means for you

> *"It is not what you do for your children, but what you have taught them to do for themselves, that will make them successful human beings."*
> Ann Landers

So how do you get your kids to take more responsibility? After all, that's what you want, and it's what they want, right? Can kids even do this?

As it turns out, they can. However, one of the most pervasive myths in our culture today is that we are entitled to a great life and that someone else is responsible for the quality of our lives. Guess what, we're not! We all must take full responsibility for everything that is experienced in life, and so must your kids. These include all areas of our lives e.g. financial, career, free time, fitness and health, relationships, personal goals and community and charity work. This book focuses on the career aspect but its principles will have an impact on all the other areas of life as well.

I'm not saying it's easy; it's not for many people. This is because many of us have been conditioned to blame ourselves, parents, bosses, the media, co-workers, the economy, the education system, the weather and our friends to name but a few. Indeed, it's easier to blame anyone and anything except ourselves. It's time to stop blaming and complaining and look inside of ourselves for the answers to our problems. It starts with how you can learn to coach your kids to take responsibility to achieve whatever they want. 100% responsibility – nothing less will do.

A personal story about responsibility

Back in 2003 I had the good fortune to work in higher education and rose through the ranks quickly. However, the world I knew and loved came crashing down in 2015 when a major restructure left me fighting for my job, which I lost to someone younger with a lack of management skills. I experienced an immense sense of loss and negativity at the time and started blaming and complaining – I can't imagine I was that nice to be around at the time. I became 'stuck' in a rut and couldn't see a way forward.

I should have known better because I had completed the Jack Canfield's Success Principles programme in 2008 as a student and later went on to become a Certified Trainer in the Success Principles, graduating in 2015 – exactly the time my career went down the pan. It was important to get back on track and so the obvious thing was to do the whole programme again with the support of other qualified trainers and coaches. One of my coaching colleagues asked me, "Are you taking 100% responsibility for what's just happened in your life?" I replied "Yes, of course", knowing that was the answer I wanted to give but it wasn't exactly true.

As the next two years unfolded I was redeployed several times into roles that needed a body in the room which basically anyone could do. Eventually I concluded that I had to take 100% responsibility for my life and career because no-one else was going to, were they?

Very soon after that realization I gave up my excuses, all my victim stories, all the reasons why I couldn't and hadn't moved on until then, and all my blaming of outside circumstances. I realized that I could use my skills and capabilities for the benefit of other people – you and your young people – by writing this book, hosting career webinars and coaching people all over the world.

Now think about your own behaviour and that of the young people in your life: when did you or they last get stuck in a rut, blame and complain about things you had no control over and become a victim of circumstances? You must give those things up forever, now, today!

Instead, you must take the position that we all have the power to change things and make them different, to make it right, to get what we want. Of course, things will get in the way: a lack of money, fear, focus, a vision for the future. All that matters whilst you work through this book is that there is a choice and if you choose to be 100% responsible you can work through anything life presents to you.

If your plans, or lack of plans, don't turn out the way you thought, then ask yourself "What do I need to do differently next time to get the result I want?"

Let's start with thinking about how you can take more responsibility for the outcomes in your life by completing the first exercise. I suggest the young people in your life also complete the exercise, which will give them the ability to take responsibility for themselves and their actions.

EXERCISE 1:
Taking 100% responsibility

As I said earlier, it's up to you to take 100% responsibility for your life. So, the question is – are you willing to do this and start to take small steps to achieve it? You have the power to choose whether to take 100% responsibility. Let's get started. I'd like you to complete the exercise below and complete the statements which will identify areas where you could take more responsibility.

If I were to take 5% more responsibility for my work and career

I would _____

If I were to take 5% more responsibility for my finances

I would _____

If I were to take 5% more responsibility for creating more recreation and free time

I would _____

If I were to take 5% more responsibility for the success of my health and fitness

I would _____

If I were to take 5% more responsibility for the level of my relationships

I would _____

If I were to take 5% more responsibility for achieving my personal goals

I would _____

If I were to take 5% more responsibility for my contribution to my community

I would _____

So, following this exercise, what is the first step you're going to take?

_____

_____

Thanks for doing the exercise. This is great news, because now there's a real chance that change can happen. A chance for you and the young people in your life to get the support and inspiration they need, a chance that will undoubtedly boost your confidence, and a chance that wasn't even there a year ago. And remember:

> *"A journey of a thousand miles begins with a single step."*
> Lao Tzu

CHAPTER 2

Grades – Who Cares? How to Find Out What You Love to Do

After reading the first chapter, you now know how important it is to take 100% responsibility. You've learnt what you and your kids can do differently, and you've completed a short exercise to get started.

The natural next step would be to go and inspire your kids to understand what their purpose in life is – why they are here on earth. You might even discover or rediscover yours at the same time! Your purpose in life is as much a part of this process as anything else, and if you're going to get good results for your kids you need to be aware of your own needs and wants as a human being.

Finding out your purpose in life takes time and is an important step towards leading a successful life. The process can be a minefield, especially in today's fast-paced world where it's easy to get sidetracked. It's easy to wander and drift and get demoralized. You may be tempted to stay on the same path – that's OK if that's what you want – but you're reading this book because you want more for you and your children, right?

The truth, however, is that many people are not fortunate enough to go through this process, but you are! A solid, simple purpose in life will work far better at increasing your kid's passion and enthusiasm for what they do and keeping them focused on their future, and that's what we want for them in the long run – to be happy and successful people.

This will seem a little daunting, but don't worry; the rest of the book after this chapter is devoted to the concept of how you and the young people in your life can get in touch with what they want from life. The danger is that you try to influence your young people throughout this process so I'm asking you, "Whose life is it anyway?"

I mention this because you may be tempted to place your own thoughts, influences and behaviours on your young people. This is not the object of the exercise. Instead try to take a step back and focus your efforts on exploring what your child wants instead. What they want is likely to be different than what you want for them, so please bear this in mind when working through the exercises.

Now I'd like to help you to discover your child's purpose in life and potentially your own – are you ready? Remember that these exercises are best done with young people age 14+ as this is the time when the family unit starts to think about further education at college and university. In addition, this exercise is equally valuable for your older children age 18+, with or without help.

> *"Everything in life has a purpose, there are no mistakes, no coincidences."*
> Elisabeth Kübler-Ross

I've already mentioned that without a purpose in life, it's easy to get sidetracked or lost. It's therefore easy to wander and drift and accomplish little in life. As I said in the last chapter, I've known hundreds of students like this who have attended college and university without any idea of why they are there or what they want to accomplish in life.

Having a purpose is an integral part of life for me. It's by no means the most important thing in life but to be 'on purpose' means that I'm doing what I love to do, doing what I'm good at and accomplishing what's important to me. Both people and things have gravitated towards me, helping me to help others, for which I am truly grateful. I'd now like to share with you what I believe my purpose in life is.

> *"My life purpose is to use my creativity and experience to support and inspire others through teaching, mentoring and coaching anywhere in the world and have fun doing it."*
> Lesley Strachan

Brian Tracy, who is one of America's leading authorities in the development of human potential and personal effectiveness, is quoted as saying:

> *"Decide upon your major definite purpose in life and then organize all your activities around it."*

The key therefore is to get your purpose in life done well, so that all your efforts are focused on it. Plain and simple!

So why is having a purpose in life important?

It's a good question: having a purpose in life is like having a compass to guide you on your journey. Ships don't leave a harbour without being able to navigate to their destination, do they? If you're going on holiday most people would work out how they're going to get there. So why not apply the same principles to life?

If a planned approach is not for you or your kids, what is? The secret to getting from where you are to where you want to be lies in this book, so you've got nothing to lose by trying some ideas out, have you?

Let's look at some ideas to get started and find out how to build your very own life purpose statement.

Life purpose: ask your kids what they want. Ask yourself what you want. The two things are likely to be different because this exercise isn't about you or what you want for them; it's about you as individuals. You are likely to want different things from life and that's OK.

In general, there is also a conversation to be had with your kids well before they start choosing subjects to study at school, college or university. In a relaxed, informal environment ask them these questions:

EXERCISE 2:
What do you love to do?

"What would be the job you'd love so much that you'd do for free but that you could actually get paid for?"

"Think back over all the things you've done so far in your life – what made you the happiest?"

For example, I have always loved dance and teaching. I would do it for free – and often have – but I also got paid for it. What makes me happy is when people say that I have inspired them; that gives me great happiness.

One young lady aged 15 that I mentor at a school in Southampton told me she loved photography and interior design, engineering and business but couldn't choose between them. So I said "Why do you have to choose – couldn't you do all of them in a future career?" She hadn't thought that was possible and was at the point of dropping some of the subjects she really loved to do and was passionate about.

Make a note of the conversations you have with your young people in preparation for the exercises you complete in the later chapters of this book. Or what I generally do is have people draw or cut out pictures to visually represent what makes them happy. Initially people will produce pictures of large expensive cars, houses and places to visit abroad. Then comes what really makes them happy, for example, friends, family and pets etc.

This should be a relatively easy exercise for very young people because they know exactly what they want and declare it: "I want that toy!" "I want to go out and play with my friends!" "I want to be a footballer!" Adolescents may find it more challenging because they start to receive tremendous interference and pressure from authority figures telling them how they should think, behave and feel.

Often older, more 'mature' people (including our parents) have totally forgotten what it is to identify what they want, declare it bravely and fight for it. Because they've lost that ability to figure out what they want. Our highest guide in all things should be ourselves, and parents who can't see that often do us a great disservice in how they raise us. Finally, in adulthood, our ability to see what we want clearly gets even more muddled, when there are so many new, competing demands that make a mess of our desires.

I want to say right now that this book is not about being selfish. It's about becoming a better person and following a path that fulfils you. Wouldn't you be a better person to live with if you were happy and fulfilled?

Many personal development leaders tell us that what we think and believe will bring into being what appears in our lives. If you think you can't have a great job that you love that also makes you a great living, then you will have exactly what you think: a lousy job you don't like that doesn't pay enough. If all you think about is what you don't have, then you'll perpetuate your lack and your unhappiness.

I work with hundreds of young people and professionals each year who want to have better, happier lives. However, what they don't see is how they have been influencing and thwarting their careers every day by fear-based negativity, anger and resentment, along with a victim mentality.

What do you want to change? Start monitoring your thoughts very carefully. Choose to think more positively and powerfully about what your future can hold and what you're capable of. The past reflects what you thought and believed and how you acted in the past.

Change your thoughts and beliefs so that they align with your most positive dreams and visions. Then take brave, concrete action that supports those visions. Greater awareness equals greater choice. And becoming braver means you'll have greater power to affect positive change in your kid's life.

I'm now going to get you to do three exercises for yourself, and then do them with the young people in your life. Young people tend to need some help with this exercise.

EXERCISE 3:
Explore your personal qualities

List two of your unique personal qualities. If you're not sure what I mean, type in the words 'unique personal qualities' into a search engine and you'll get a list of various sources that you can use to determine your own personal qualities. They can be qualities like: Sincere, Honest, Loyal, Friendly, Reliable, Helpful, Creative etc.

HINT: It's sometimes helpful to have each of the personal qualities on stick it notes or cards so that you can move them around to prioritise the most important ones.

1. _____

2. _____

List one or two ways you enjoy expressing those qualities when interacting with others such as to inspire or to support.

Personal Quality #1   **Personal Quality #2**

_____   _____

_____   _____

_____   _____

Then have your kids do the same exercise. They may have similar qualities to you and equally they may express different qualities. It's important for both of you to recognize and value each other's personal qualities and not try to influence each other's responses.

Let's assume for a moment that your world is everything you want it to be right now (work with me on this one). Why is it perfect for you? What are you doing? How are you feeling? Where are you? When did the world become perfect for you? Who are you with?

Write your thoughts down in the present tense. I found this exercise very powerful and at the same time unbelievable because at the time I did it I wasn't sure I could achieve something close to my perfect world. I'm sharing my own thoughts with you to help you through the exercise.

My example: "My world is perfect right now because I am doing a job that I love. I am an award-winning coach, consultant, adviser, speaker and trainer and travel all over the world for work and pleasure. I am feeling content and proud to be part of my own and other people's transformations. I am based in Southampton in the UK and work from home and my dog Ben is a great companion. I also travel extensively and ended up writing this book on planes and trains because that's where I got loads of spare time to write. My world became much better when I eventually decided to take severance from the organization I had worked in for 14 years. I am now running a successful business working for myself with the support of my family and friends and having the time of my life. I am also rediscovering my love and passion for dancing which is helping me to keep fit and healthy."

Now it's your turn… do the same exercise for yourself and/or with the young people in your life. It's a good idea to communicate with each other and share your hopes and dreams which will help you to understand each other better.

EXERCISE 4:
What is your perfect world?

_____

My world is perfect right now because:

_____

_____

_____

_____

_____

Now combine all your responses into a single statement. An example from my personal statement is, "My purpose is to use my extensive experience to inspire others through teaching, mentoring and coaching all over the world and have fun doing it." Everything I do daily is focused on what I want to do and it makes saying NO to people a lot easier.

There are many ways to define your purpose. I learnt this method from Jack Canfield during my training as a Certified Trainer in the Success Principles. You could choose to use a different method of defining your life purpose. Try to construct your own purpose statement below.

EXERCISE 5:
My purpose in life

My purpose is to:

_____

_____

_____

_____

_____

_____

_____

So, you've defined your purpose in life; what now? You might want to make a visual representation of your purpose. For example, why not grab loads of pictures, words and symbols and make a vision board? You could then hang it hang it somewhere where you'll see it a lot e.g. in the kitchen, bathroom, in your office, as a screensaver or in the hallway. The idea is that wherever you hang it you will see it often to remind you. This will keep you focused on your purpose in life.

As we move forward with other exercises which will define your vision and goals, make sure you have your purpose in life at the forefront of your mind because your vision and goals should be aligned to your purpose in life. And that's it.

It might seem a bit overwhelming to you, so take one step at a time; you don't have to do all the exercises in one go. It may take days, weeks or months. You may want to revisit the exercises several times before you're happy with your statement. One thing is for sure: you have a purpose in life and so do your children. The objective in this chapter is to articulate it and then plan everything you do around it.

This exercise is also particularly helpful for individuals who tell me that they are not settled in their job, can't find a job that they are passionate about or can't tell me why they are studying for their degree courses. It's also valuable for people facing severance and redundancy as this exercise gets people back in touch with who they are.

Whilst I have given you work-related examples here, the concept applies to every part of our lives. So, my question to you is, "Are you living a purposeful, fulfilled and passionate life; are you happy?" If you are then you can stop reading now; if not, read on because there are good reasons why having a purpose if life is literally 'good for you'.

The need for purpose is one of the defining characteristics of human beings. Human beings can suffer psychological difficulties when they don't have a purpose in life. This is discussed further in an article by Steve Taylor called The Power of Purpose in *Psychology Today*[2] which suggests that people who have a clear understanding of their purpose in life are less vulnerable to boredom, anxiety, depression and substance abuse. Alcohol or drugs are, of course, a way of alleviating psychological discord, but at the same time they can be seen as a way of gaining a very negative sense of purpose: to satisfy the addiction.

On the other hand, a purpose can have a powerful and positive effect on your life. When you have a sense of purpose, you never get up in the morning wondering what you're going to do with yourself. When you're 'on purpose' life becomes easier, less complicated and less stressful. You become more mono-focused, like an arrow flying towards its target, and your mind feels somehow taut and strong, with less space for negativity to seep in.

If you've not read Victor Frankl's famous book called *Man's Search for Meaning*, it's well worth a read. In the book Frankl describes his experiences in concentration camps during the Second World War. Frankl observed that the inmates who were most likely to survive were those who felt they had a goal or purpose. Frankl himself spent a lot of time trying to reconstruct a manuscript he had lost on his journey to the camp – his life's work. Others held on to a vision of their future – seeing their loved ones again or a major task to complete once they were free.

No-one really knows why having a purpose has such a positive effect and there are many different reasons why a strong purpose in life is good for our mental health. Some writers say that having a purpose makes us less prone to what I call 'psychological discord'. This is the fundamental sense of unease we often experience which can manifest itself in boredom, anxiety and depression.

If we have a purpose and channel our mental energies it gives us a constant source of activity to focus on. This means there is less likelihood of spending time on the negative chatter which often triggers negative thoughts and feelings. Another important factor to be considered is that aligning ourselves to a purpose often makes us less self-centred. We feel a part of something bigger, something outside ourselves, and this makes us less focused on our own worries and anxieties. Our own problems seem less significant, and we spend less time thinking about them, and so our sense of wellbeing and happiness increases.

Having a sense of purpose can also enhance our self-esteem. This is because if we are successfully dealing with the challenges that come our way and moving that bit closer to our goal we feel better and hopeful. Research shows that hope has a positive effect on how we feel, and the effect is evident especially with people who are suffering any form of long-term illness. For them, a high level of hope brings both an increased ability to cope, and an increased chance of recovery.

Some people will find working through the exercises in this book overwhelming. For others it will be plain sailing. Either way I want you to step back and take things one step at a time. Think of these exercises as a giant jigsaw which you're completing one piece at a time.

Stuff to be aware of:

- Please do not overcomplicate these exercises; go with your gut feeling and thoughts that pass through your mind. If nothing comes to mind that's OK too; wait until something comes to you.
- Don't lose heart when designing your life purpose statement; it's simply a tool to help you to get in touch with who you are and what you want.
- Overcomplicated is never better: simple is best here!
- Life purpose statements are a vital part of your life so do take your time and revisit your statement regularly.

So, you've got the basic idea of a life purpose statement – or you might not have at this point. If you find that you prefer someone like a coach to inspire and motivate you then there are some ideas later about how to find the coach for you.

CHAPTER 3

What Do You Want from Life?

Having a life purpose statement is all well and good, but it doesn't do much for you if you don't know what you want. I'll get you to a place where you're clearer about what you want, and I'll do this using targeted exercises. I'm not going to make this a complicated exercise, but it is an important concept to understand. This is because to get what you want out of life you need to decide what it is you want. So, what do you (or your young people) want?

The key questions I suggest you ask now are:

- What do you want from life?
- What does your future life look like, feel like, sound like; what's happening?
- Who do you want to be?
- What do you want to have?

If this is too difficult and confusing, make a list of what you don't want first. I originally found writing down what I wanted difficult, but it became much easier when I wrote down what I didn't want on the left-hand side of a page and then thought: "If I don't want that, what do I want instead?" This made the exercise much easier for me personally. This exercise works well with teenagers.

During coaching sessions, I often find that people haven't defined clearly what they want because what they want has become secondary to the needs of others. We didn't start off life like that, did we? Look at the behaviour of babies and young children. They know exactly what they want and how to get it. As the years go by they become influenced by their parents, peers, teachers, careers advisers, marriage, divorce, changes of circumstances and so the list goes on.

Throughout life we hear other people say to us:

- Don't do that.
- You'll never be able to that.
- You can't be a doctor.
- Your children come first.
- This is not the right time.
- You should stay and make it work.
- It's too late to go back to studying.
- You're too old now.

As we become affected by what other people say, some of us lose sight of who we are and what we wanted from life in the first place. That's happened to me, and it happens to all of us at different stages of our lives. That said, it is possible to get back on track if you are 100% committed. My advice to you to is not to live someone else's dream, or try to get your kids to live your dreams.

Encourage them to design their own life and not be influenced by external or family influences. Coach young people to explore their own purpose in life, let them be who they are, encourage them to find their passion in life and support them without offering your own opinion about what they should do.

My question to you is, "Are you settling for something less than you want?"

If you are settling for less than what you want, you may want to think about the language you use daily. Try to become aware of what you say and how you say it. For example:

- I can't go out because I must care for my...
- I should work today even though it's my day off.
- I ought to clean the house, car, windows but I'm so tired.
- I can't let the kids walk to school; it's too dangerous.

My ultimate favourite which I often hear from young people is **whatever**, or **I don't know**, or they simply shrug their shoulders. Many parents, guardians and teachers will recognize one or more of these reactions.

The statement that bothered me the most when I taught in a university was "My parents said I had to go to university, but I don't want to be here. I wanted to work in the film industry." Then this young person started to cry. Her situation is not an isolated case. She was frustrated by trying to please her parents but really upset that she wasn't being allowed or supported to follow her passions and enthusiasm. She felt that she didn't have a choice and that she felt obliged to follow the path her parents had laid down for her.

After completing the exercises in this book, she evolved into a completely different person. I've never seen such a change in behaviour, posture, attitude or self-confidence when this young lady had been through this process. She started to apply for work experience and internships in her field of study (film). She was encouraged to go back to her old school and college and offer to film some events, which she did. This work started the beginning of a work portfolio for her and eventually led to some temporary work in the film industry. It just goes to show – never say never. She is at least a few steps further forward on her journey than she was this time last year and that's what I call progress.

I often find people say that they don't have a choice. In the end everyone has a choice about what and how they say things, what decisions are made, and whether they prioritize themselves or others. Now you might be saying, "It's not that easy." Sometimes if it's a big decision it's not that easy and you'll need to take one tiny step at a time. For other, smaller decisions, try to form new habits.

For example: if your kids are old enough to get on a bus to come home from school, why do you drop everything and go and pick them up in the car? It's an old habit which you could stop and you could start to form new habits if you wanted to. I stopped doing the school run when my son went to secondary school because there was a school bus he could use. The extra time I gained allowed me to do other things that I preferred to do. He also gained some independence which many young people don't now have these days for all sorts of reasons.

Here's another example. A friend of mine does nothing but moan about her kids on Facebook. They've left the fridge door open again, they won't tidy their rooms, they both demand different meals, they won't do their homework, they demand that their mother drives around taking them here, there and everywhere in between.

I asked my friend "Whose problem is this, Jane?" She stopped and looked at me and then told me all the reasons she had to do everything she did for her kids. So, I asked the question again: "Whose problem is this, Jane?" After a while she decided not to pick up all their clothes, wash, iron and return them to their drawers, and instead left everything where it was. She left a note under their doors with instructions on how to use the washing machine.  To be fair there was an uproar to begin with, but the kids have now got the hang of what to do and the experience has taught them valuable life skills for when they eventually leave home and run their own home.

So, now to the good bit. Getting back to the subject of making choices about life – the next step is to clarify what you really want and the best way to do this is to make a list. You can do the list by yourself or with a friend. Working with a friend is a great way to get the ball rolling because the other person can just keep saying "What do you want?" over and over. They can also write down the answers for you, which gives you time to think deeply about what you really want.

This is a great exercise to do with your kids as well. Interestingly, some young people will say "I don't know." If this happens, ask them: "OK, but if you did know what you wanted, what does that look like?"

EXERCISE 6:
Make an 'I want' list

One of the easiest ways to start clarifying what you really want is to make a list of 10 things you want to do, 10 things you want to have and 10 things you want to be before you die (also called a bucket list). This is a great way to get the ball rolling.

Another technique to unearth your wants is to ask a friend to help you make an 'I want' list. Have your friend continually ask, "What do you want?" over and over for about 10-15 minutes. You'll probably find that what you want isn't that profound!

If you find that you have many more things to write down, simply extend the list until you run out of ideas.

Things I want to do	Things I want to have	Things I want to be
e.g. Visit China	e.g. A flat of my own	e.g. fulfilled

Chapter 3: What Do You Want from Life?

It doesn't matter if you can't think of 10 things for each category right now. Come back to it another time. In the meantime, your brain will keep working on it and you'll have some of those aha moments when you least expect it.

And as I said, some things on the lists won't be that profound either. After you've listed the dream house and car, it's more likely the simpler things in life will surface. I wanted more time to do the things I wanted to do instead of working 60 hours a week and I wanted to be appreciated sometimes. I wanted to be happier, start dancing again, write a book etc. So, I had to make changes to my lifestyle to do it.

To change my lifestyle, I knew I had to make some hard decisions. As I alluded to earlier, in 2015 I was part of a major restructuring exercise where I worked. We all had to re-apply for our jobs and the number of positions we were all applying for was reduced by half. I didn't get the job I had been successfully doing for 14 years so after two years of psyching myself up and working with a coach I decided to apply for the severance package that was on offer at work.

Having been a teacher, trainer and coach, I decided to go back to working for myself again. I now work and collaborate with the most amazing people in the world. I love what I do, and when I recently went back and looked at my vision board I was excited to see that I had achieved most of my goals. Five years ago, I would never have dreamed that I would have the life I now have and that it would be so different. It's never too late to make real changes in your life.

So, how are your three lists coming along? Lists are great; we make them all the time. However, when I work with clients, I generally see three mistakes almost every time when we start talking about what they want:

1. Initially people are very excited to share with us what they want – and please share yours on my Facebook page, Lesley Strachan Consulting and Training (http://bit.ly/LesleyFB). However sometimes it's tough for me to say that unless you're 100% committed to the process your lists are just that – lists.

2. The things clients want can't happen unless action is taken to make it happen. You must take action, however large or small, to get what you really want; otherwise it's just a wish list.

3. Then there's the belief that it's not possible, or that you feel unworthy, so you start to question yourself, like "How can I afford to do that?", "How is that even possible?", "What will my family think?", "Am I really capable of doing that?" or "If I go back to school, I won't be accepted!"

As a rule, these thoughts are just that – thoughts. Do you know what the letters in the word FEAR stand for?

FALSE **E**VIDENCE **A**PPEARING **R**EAL!

The most important thing to remember is to feel the fear and do it anyway. Susan Jeffers wrote a great book on the subject called *Feel the Fear and Do It Anyway* which is worth a read when you get some time to yourself! Letting fear overcome you is a trap that many people fall into all the time, and you've got to watch out for it. Even I'm not immune to it on occasions.

Think back to when you were very small or ask your family and friends what you were like as a baby, and later as a child. Were you fearful then? Did you take risks, try something new? Listen to what they say, and you might be surprised. I asked my mum what I was like as a child and she said, "You were always very smiley and chatty, a really happy baby." She gave me a photo of me at around two years old which you can see on the right, and when I saw that picture I thought  to myself, "Where has she gone?" I had these thoughts at some of the lowest points in my life and there have been a few. The point is that we all must keep reminding ourselves of who we are despite the difficult times we all face at one time or another.

The reason this works is because it gets into your mind to remind or rediscover the real you! Your friends and family probably have a different view of who you are and sometimes it's good to hear a different perspective. This might be a little overwhelming, but don't worry, I'm not saying that you must nail this on the first try. It's not the end of the world because you can modify, refine or come back to this whenever you want to.

What it comes down to is this: to get what you want, you must know what you want to have, be and do. Focus on taking one small step at a time and accept 100% responsibility for taking the action you need to take, or a huge step if you'd prefer.

Find something that works for you and makes you happier.

So, where are you going to start?

How about setting some short, medium and long-term goals and sticking to them?

Remember that Rome wasn't built in a day! For example: if you want more time for yourself – how will you do this? What must change? When will you do this by? Pick something you can have an early success with to build up your confidence to begin with, then with the wind in your sails get cracking on the next thing on your list because a ship in harbour is safe – but that's not what ships are built for.

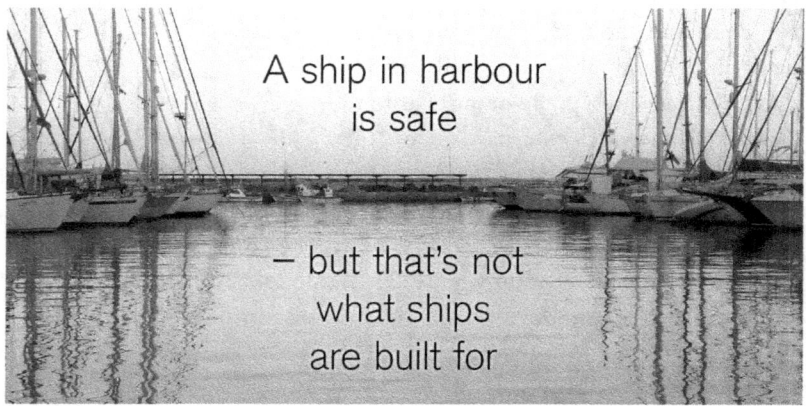

⚠ WARNING:

Don't overdo it! Work on some things on your list where you can get some early quick wins, then something which will take some time, and then something long term. Try not to attack the whole list in one go because you may lose your motivation. I always ask the lovely people I work with to consider putting aside 30 minutes a week as a strategy to get started on their lists – can you commit to that?

Another very, very important thing to think about is a strategy for getting things on your list done. Of all your three lists and all the things you want, what are your priorities?

EXERCISE 7:
My top 3 priorities and why

If you had to choose your top 3 today, what would they be and why? Repeat the same exercise with your young people.

1. _____

2. _____

3. _____

Once you've decided what you want in clear compelling detail, it's time to step up your game. Now we're going to get into what you love doing in life!

Preparation for the next chapter

- Don't worry right now about earning money to make a living – we'll get to that later!
- Look back at the two identified personal qualities again and make a note of them.
- In a moment you're going to find out, or rediscover, what you love to do and see whether you could create a living out of something you are passionate about. Sound exciting?
- Remember to do this part with your young people as well.
- Be natural! Don't try to be something you're not at this point.

CHAPTER 4

Let's Find Out What You Love to Do

If you've been following this book thus far, you've got a reasonable understanding of yourself, and maybe your kids have too. In fact, you're probably better off than anybody who just went off on a short course and then got back to real life. This is because the majority of that learning never gets implemented and the notes go in the drawer never to be seen again.

You're definitely better off than anyone who has refused to think about what they want from life, and honour what they love to do. You may even have pulled a few ideas from our work so far and be considering implementing them.

I like your style but hold on to your seat – your work is not over yet! In this chapter, you're going to figure out how to find out what you love to do and make money out of it, if money is a key driver for you. It was for me, as I have bills to pay as well!

Is making money a key driver for you now?

We all need to make money to make ends meet, don't we? This need often stops people from following their hopes and aspirations because they believe that they can't make a living from them. Maybe you can't, but wouldn't it be great to at least explore the possibilities and potential?

Here are a few examples to think about:

Many of our best loved celebrities didn't start off with the career they ended up with:

- Robin Williams trained as an actor before moving into comedy where he excelled at doing something he loved.
- The actor Harrison Ford was a carpenter before he was an actor.
- Vera Wang was a figure skater and journalist before going into the fashion industry in her forties and becoming a fashion designer.
- The singer Sting was a teacher before going into the music industry.

You get the idea – don't you? It's never too late to follow your passion and do what you love to do.

To inspire you to find out what you love to do, I suggest that you make a list of 20 things you love to do, and then think of ways to make a living doing some of those things. Your kids should do the same exercise either with you or on their own. Swap lists to get a better understanding of each other!

Here are some examples to help you:

- If you love sport, you could play, be a sports writer, sports photographer, coach or go into sports management.
- If you love music, you could be a singer, songwriter, agent, writer of music, work in the music industry or a music shop, put your songs online or work in a theatre.
- If you love to help people, you could work for the third sector, volunteer at home or abroad, help your community, teach or work with the elderly.

You get the idea? Now do this exercise.

EXERCISE 8:
Exploring what you love to do

What I love to do	Ways of making a living

I hope by the time you've done this exercise you've discovered or rediscovered what you love to do and have thought about how you could make money out of doing what you love to do! How did your kids get on with this exercise? What did you learn about them? Tell me on Facebook at Lesley Strachan Consulting and Training (http://bit.ly/LesleyFB).

The next step

You might have noticed that the theme of this book is focused on getting you from where you are to where you want to be. The fact of the matter is, however, that you must know two things:

- Where you are
- Where you want to get to

To get to where you want to be, you need to be able to envisage your future and to plan what your desired outcome will be – your vision of your future.

Having a vision of your future also has one distinct advantage for us in that it's by far the easiest, most convenient, and most effective way to express what you want from life. You don't have to change it all the time; you just need to update your vision every now and then.

It's especially helpful to know that there's no 'magic bullet' or fast-track way get you from where you are now to where you want to get to, and that slow and steady wins the race. I talked earlier about allocating 30 minutes a week to get started on your lists – slow and steady. If you can move quicker, go for it, remembering that in either case you must take 100% responsibility – always.

This may seem daunting at first, and understandably so; the thought of having to take 100% responsibility and act by implementing your ideas isn't appealing to everyone. If you truly think about it, however, once a week isn't too bad; that's only four times a month. Also, if you make a schedule and stick to it you'll find that implementing your ideas really isn't the chore you thought it would be.

If you're finding that you have time for more, it's beneficial for you to up your hours from 30 minutes to 60 minutes a week; that's the optimal number in this sort of situation, and it'll most likely net you the most positive impact on making the changes you want to make. Any more than that and you may find yourself overwhelmed and become demotivated if things don't move as fast as you'd like them to. Besides, there are other, better things you could be doing with that time!

CHAPTER 5

Let's Get to the Point: Clarifying Your Vision of Your Ideal Life

---

You might be wary at this point. You might be sitting in your home or office, having read the title of this chapter, and be thinking "Clarifying my vision! That can't possibly help me."

Don't laugh just yet; I know how silly the word 'vision' sounds. I know the derision it's received from all sides, including our friends and the media, but the fact of the matter is that your vision of your future is relevant. As much as it pains me to say, your vision may be one of the more important factors that figures in your life.

So, let's get to work!

Why a vision?

Simply put: your vision is a detailed description of where you want to get to. It describes in detail what your destination looks like and feels like.

To create a balanced and successful life, you vision is likely to include the following seven areas:

- Work and career
- Finances
- Recreation and free time
- Health and fitness
- Relationships
- Personal goals
- And contribution to the larger community

At this stage it isn't necessary to know exactly how you're going to achieve your vision. All that's important right now is that you figure out where you want to get to. If you get clear on the why, the how will be taken care of.

In this chapter, we're going to look at how to approach your own vision of where you want to be and use it to help you get there!

There are different ways of responding to the questions in all seven sections. You might want to write down your answers as you go. Or you could do the whole exercise first whilst using meditation or relaxation techniques. Whichever way you choose, make sure you capture your future state by writing down everything as soon as you complete each of the seven exercises.

Each day I suggest you review the vision you have written down. This could be in the form of a colourful pictorial vision board which you could hang somewhere you'll see it often and at least daily. Mobile phones are also a great place to store your vision.

1. Work and career

In this section, we're going to focus on what you'd prefer to be doing at work, or in your career. This isn't to say you should ignore your current work situation; it's still important, and you need to be present at work whilst moving forward with your plans. You still probably need to earn money to live?

In the meantime, I want you to watch a film which stars you as the lead character. Watch, hear and act as if you were already in your new role or career. Get into your character. Who are you working with? What are you doing? Where are you working? When did you start the new role?
How does it feel? Why did you choose this new job or career? This focus on living and acting as if you are already doing the job will give you a positive feeling of success. Write a script for yourself if that helps.

2. Finances

Your finances are one of the most important aspects to consider. Everybody needs money to live and you're going to capitalize on that now. The first thing you should have is a firm idea of how much you want to earn and link those thoughts to the work and career sections you've just completed in the previous section. So, let's imagine you are now where you want to be and have the job and career you've dreamed about.

💡 TIP:

You may fear this exercise for different reasons. You might find the process of thinking in big numbers a bit scary – I did at first. It's very important to note that your finances are personal to you and whatever you decide to think about is your business.

EXERCISE 9:
Planning your career

Let's get started then. Remembering that you are now living and working in your new job or career, give as much detail as you can:

How much are you earning in your new job or career? How long have you had this new job?

Which country are you living in? How did that happen?

Where are you living now? Describe your house in detail.

What kind of car do you drive – describe your lifestyle. Do you need materials things now?

Where are you going on holiday now? Explain the kinds of places you are visiting.

How much do you have in investments and property? Do you have a financial adviser?

---

3. Recreation and free time

So far, you've described yourself in your new reality in the areas of work, career and finances. You may well understand the time pressures we put upon ourselves and the pressure others put upon us, whether they are perceived or real.

To manage a balanced lifestyle (if that's what you're aiming for) we're now going to explore what you're doing in the area of recreation and free time. This section is sometimes difficult for people. I want to share my own experience with you. I absolutely love what I do 100% and find resting hard. I work hard and know I must take time off to rest and get my energy levels back up to their normal levels, so this is how I do it.

I plan long weekends away, and annual holidays, often a year ahead. The dates get booked into my diary and the holidays happen, no excuses, and work is turned away. I deliberately make myself unavailable. The reason I make myself unavailable is because I could continue to work and burn out. That's happened to me before, and then I'm no use to anyone. Does that sound familiar?

Even if you have a small income and can't book holidays away, you can take time off work, and go out for the day somewhere; you don't have to spend any money. Some of my friends often take a day off, stay in their pajamas and watch movies all day to chill and relax.

EXERCISE 10:

How do you spend your free time?

Imagine now that you have found the job or career of your dreams. I'd like you to think in the present tense again as if you have achieved your goals. Close your eyes and watch the film of yourself again as we did previously. Write down answers to the following questions:

What are you doing in your recreation and free time?

In the free time you've created, what are you doing with your family and friends?

What hobbies or interests have you taken up, or do you do more of?

What kinds of short breaks, or holidays, do you go on now?

How do you have fun in your new life?

What is different in your new life compared to your old life?

The great part of experiencing these changes in the present tense is that your brain consciously and subconsciously starts to work on what you want. At this point you might want to cut out some pictures from magazines or download some visuals ready for an exercise coming up later. Share them with us on Facebook as well.

Visualizing the future is sometimes a massive leap forward for many people, for many reasons. Psychologically, it's a helpful way to increase personal aspirations and passion and motivation. Also, if you find yourself in a negative mental space, visualizing will enable you to think more positively, giving you an aim in life. It's the right exercise to be doing to get in touch with what you want. Don't forget to have your young people do this exercise either with you or on their own.

It was interesting working with one young lady this year who said, "I really liked to cook with my mum, but we don't do it anymore because of exam preparation." So, we came to an agreement that once a week she would take a couple of hours from her studies to do what she loved to do – cook and chat to her mum. Since then the young lady involved has been happier and less stressed.

Once you've got your recreation and free time sorted out it's time to move on!

4. Health and fitness

Health and fitness is one of the biggest businesses out there – and perhaps one that inspires most of us to act or puts us off doing anything. There are endless magazines, articles and TV programmes related to health and fitness, and whether we like it or not the fact remains that our health and fitness is important: they are the two things that will help us to lead a full and productive life.

EXERCISE 11:
Your health and fitness

Let's see how your health and fitness stacks up:

TIP:
Remember to visualize your ideal health and fitness.

What is your ideal vision of your body and your physical health?

What weight are you?

Are you free of disease?

What's your predicted life span?

Are you happy and relaxed all day?

_____

What are your energy levels like?

_____

Are you flexible and strong in your mind and body?

_____

How much exercise do you engage in?

_____

Do you eat what nutritionists consider to be good food?

_____

Do you drink lots of water?

_____

What's your alcohol intake per week?

_____

Do you get enough rest and sleep?

_____

The answers to these questions are so important. Every single answer contributes to your overall health and fitness. If you've noticed any areas where you might make some changes, take advantage of this knowledge and set yourself some realistic goals today. What did your kids come up with?

This may seem daunting especially if you have big goals and/or a long list of things on your to do list. Truth be told, however, if you take one tiny step at a time you'll find it easier than trying to do everything at the same time. You can sit down for an hour and write enough small goals for a week or two, schedule them, and forget about them until the next week when you sit down to write some more!

Don't be tempted to implement everything on your list; break it down to what you know you can do. For example, most of us don't eat five portions of vegetables or fruit every day. What you can do, however, is have another 100g every now and then, or make a commitment to yourself (100% responsibility) to replace a chocolate bar with a piece of fruit. Yeah, I struggle with that one, but you know the old saying, don't you?

"YOU ARE WHAT YOU EAT."

My job in this book is to heighten your awareness of these areas in your life. Your job is to take 100% responsibility for any changes you want to make and implement them.

Take advantage of the time you're spending reading and implementing the concepts in this book to generate a new future for yourself and your kids. It's a great tool for slowly and steadily creating the links between where you are now and where you want to be.

5. Relationships

In this section, we will review the relationships you have with your family, friends and co-workers. Sometimes relationships are completely overshadowed by a change in circumstances that can have an impact on both you and the other person(s). Close your eyes if you want to and watch another film of what your ideal relationships are. Sometimes relationships are completely overshadowed by bigger priorities like finances, your job, your free time and your health and fitness as a few examples. You can probably think of more.

EXERCISE 12:
Your relationships

___

Consider your responses to the following questions (remember that you're imaging your ideal future relationships):

What is your relationship with your family and friends?

___

Who are your friends?

___

What is the quality of your relationships with your friends?

___

What do those friendships feel like?

___

Are your friends like-minded, supportive and good to be around?

_____

What kinds of things are you enjoying doing with your friends and family?

_____

Are the relationships with friends and family different in this future state than they are currently, and if so, how are they different?

_____

If you decide to make changes to your life and start working towards what you really want, you may need the support of your family and friends. So, if you feel that these relationships need to be fostered right now, consider making changes immediately.

Relationships are often regarded as 'just there' and they don't need to be worked on; this is a big mistake for many of us. Our relationships can be a great source of support if we nurture and value them. For example, parents can often be a source of support because of their own life experiences; partners can often be a helpful listening post; friends can often help us to see things from a different perspective; co-workers can also be a valuable support mechanism because they're not related to us.

Put simply, try to appreciate your relationships by:

- Noticing the little things that others do and thanking them for it
- Noticing the big things and being thankful for them
- Supporting your partner's, friends' and co-workers' passions

Relationships also need to be nurtured through interacting with each other. What could you do more of, less of, or differently? The same principles apply to young people.

6. Personal goals

This isn't really what most of us think about but I'm going to incorporate it into this section because it deals with you valuing yourself as an individual. In a sense, your personal goals are as important as what everyone around you wants from you.

You may well have personal goals and be focused on achieving them. But you may not. Some people will always put their own needs and wants behind family, friends and work.

Others believe that it's selfish to put yourself before other people and may be told by others that they are selfish. These controlling messages will have an impact on whether you set and achieve your personal goals.

My question to you is: if you were happy and fulfilled would you be a happier person, and would your positive attitude then rub off onto those around you? Is that being selfish? The likelihood is you'll be in a better place mentally to help and support others.

So, let's think about you now!

EXERCISE 13:
Your ideal life

Do you want to go back to school, college or university to achieve more?

Do you want to quit your job and start a business?

Would you like to retrain in a new career area, and if so what would you do?

Will you use a coach or a mentor to help you to achieve your goals or have therapy to move through a difficult situation?

Will you meditate, go to yoga, spend time with yourself?

Will you join a club or society to take up a new hobby or interest?

Would you like to learn a musical instrument?

How about writing a book?

_____

Are you going to run a marathon?

_____

Would you like to travel, where to and why?

_____

I think you've probably got the idea reading through this list. Please feel free to add your own and let me know what they are so I can add them to the next edition.

7. Contribution to the larger community

EXERCISE 14:
Love the community you live in

We now come to the final section where we focus on the community in which you live, the community you've chosen. This may look different to the community you live in right now.

Describe the community you live in in detail. What does it look like, feel like?

What kinds of community activity takes place, and what part do you play in the community?

Are you engaged in any charitable work, and if so what is it?

What do you do to help others to make a difference to their lives?

How often do you get involved with community activities?

Who are you helping?

EXERCISE 15:
Your ideas

What else can you think of that you'd like to develop for yourself?

_____

_____

_____

_____

_____

There are both paid and free things you can do, so do some research to see if what you want is possible. The more you think about what you want in the personal area of your life the more likely it will happen because of the way the brain works, as I discussed earlier in this book. What were your kid's responses?

Your contribution to the larger community

Think about the community you live in. You may have chosen to live there but equally you might not have a choice right now. Giving back to the community is a great thing to do. I've already mentioned that I am privileged to be a business mentor for young people in one of my local schools. In this role I aim to:

- Increase confidence and self-esteem
- Increase the likelihood of them achieving their full potential
- Increase engagement in the planning of their own future
- Increase motivation and engagement
- Increase resilience

This is one example. The whole family unit could look at what kind of community activity is taking place and volunteer to help. There are great opportunities to work in the charity sector – they are always looking for people to support their causes.

EXERCISE 16:
Your community

What do you or your young people do to help others and make a difference to your local community?

If you don't currently do anything – what will you do?

Bringing this section together

You may have written down your responses as you went along, or you can do the whole exercise in one go after you've watched the film of yourself in your new life. Either way, make sure you capture everything in words or pictures as soon as you've completed each of the seven areas of your life. Your young people should also make sure they capture all their thoughts and ideas so that they remain fresh.

You will need to find a way of capturing your vision in a way that is meaningful for you.

There are many ways the future can be captured:

Mobile devices – Make a screensaver so that you see your vision whenever you look at your phone.

Video – Some people like to make a video of where they are and what they're doing. Many of my postgraduate students did this. You can watch, share, or comment on your video. It's easy to do with the camera function.

Vision or mood board – I'm sharing mine here to inspire you to do one for yourself. Visual people often like to present their ideas in pictures. Mine is in my office right next to the computer so I'm looking at it all day every day. I do have a written version to refer to once a month, but I prefer looking at pictures to motivate me.

Other places could be in the hallway at home, on the fridge door, on the wall of your office, or anywhere you pass often so that you're looking at it at least once a day or more.

Recording – If you record yourself talking in the present tense of how your life is in the future you can store the recording on your phone and listen to it every day to inspire and motivate you.

Every day – Review the vision you've written down, filmed, put in a mood or vision board or recorded. This will keep your subconscious and conscious mind focused on your vision.

As you implement the other principles and tools in this book, you will notice how your vision reveals itself. For example, there are things on my vision board I hadn't realized had already happened. It's only when I looked at it one day that I said out loud "Wow… I didn't do anything, and it happened."

Sharing your vision – To share your vision is a great thing to do. Share with a good supporting and positive friend, or a network of people you trust. However, bear in mind that your young people may not wish to share so don't force the issue now.

It might be that you imagine that the vision is too big, too wild and impossible to achieve. Other words that might pop into your mind might be: unrealistic, materialistic, or idealistic.

That's fine; we all start off that way. But the truth is, most people deep down in their core want the same things you do. Most people want money to live on, a nice home, work that they enjoy, good health, time for themselves, loving relationships and an opportunity to do good in the world.

The difference is that you've articulated it. You'll find people will want to try and help you make it happen, and you'll develop new networks of these kinds of people. Others will introduce you to people and resources that can help you. It's happened to me and it will happen to you if you implement the principles and techniques in this book.

Well done and congratulations on getting this far – so, do you believe it's possible? That's the subject of the next chapter.

CHAPTER 6

Out with the Old: How to Believe Your Vision Is Possible

"Your playing small does not serve the world. Who are you not to be great?"
Nelson Mandela

Having completed your vision of your future, you now have to believe that it is possible. Deep down, is this what you really want? There must be a deep-seated belief that the vision you have drawn together is possible. You'll recognize that little voice in your head which will tell you that it's not possible. These little voices are common so don't worry about them.

Instead, you must make the choice to believe in yourself or not. Belief is an attitude of mind and a habit. It's something that you can develop over time by changing the way you think about and react to different situations you are faced with.

Some of us are lucky enough to have loving and supporting parents who believe we can do anything. I had those kinds of parents. Thousands more people do not have those positive role models in their lives. The result is that those who cared for us during our formative years may have inadvertently passed onto us limiting beliefs and the negative conditioning they grew up with.

However, the past is where those limiting beliefs and negative conditioning should stay. There is nothing to be gained today by referring to points in our lives where we suffered from a lack of self-confidence, self-esteem, or resilience. There is nothing positive about blaming and complaining about the past because you are here now and have designed your new future.

You should now take responsibility to take charge of your own self-concepts and your beliefs. Resist the urge to fall back on past behaviours and beliefs and instead practise new ones. Here's an example:

A few years ago, I studied a great course written for coaches like me. The programme suggested the exact words I should use to send to people in my contact list to trigger a conversation about what I did. At the time I thought to myself "I can't send that, what will people think?" I procrastinated for weeks before I sent my first message.

Then I told myself "If you don't reach out and start a conversation, how are you going to enable people to become aware of your services and get new business?" I knew what I had to do but it took me months to pluck up the confidence to send the messages. In the end I had nothing to lose and everything to gain. I now send five of these messages a week, and it's become part of my normal routine of reaching out to people who may want to work with me. I haven't been told to stop or had anyone be offensive. However, I have had referral business, so it has worked well in the end.

EXERCISE 17:
One thing you will do differently

_____

What one thing will you do differently this week?

I will _____

_____

What one thing will your young people do differently this week?

I will _____

_____

Once you have a baseline for your success, test the gain further by continuing with the same activity or develop new ones. This may simply be making calls, sending emails, filling out that application form, visiting someone you haven't seen for years, trying out a new fitness class, or forgiving someone who has done you a wrong. Work towards enhancing your life because you're only here once!

So, remember that you make your own choices. Choose to believe it's possible and then act as if it's possible. Some things to try are:

- Standing up straighter, feeling taller
- Smiling more. Look in the mirror and smile at least once a day
- Acknowledging people, making eye contact and speaking to people
- Pulling your shoulders down and back towards your spine
- Speaking with more volume if you usually speak quietly

Acting as if you were the person you want to be is critical in your personal development, to build self-esteem and self-confidence. If you believe it's possible then you will do the things necessary to bring about the results you want. If you don't believe it's possible then you will not get the results you want. It becomes a self-fulfilling prophecy!

Let's take an example from competing athletes to bring home the points I'm making in the chapter. Jack J. Lesyk Ph.D from the Ohio Center for Sport Psychology suggests that what athletes have in common is that their sport is important to them and they're committed to be the best that they can be within the scope of their limitations – other life commitments, finances, time, and their natural ability.

> **EXERCISE 18:**
> What's important to you?
>
> Given the work you've done so far in this book:
>
> What's important to you?
>
> Are you committed to be the best you can be within the scope of your limitations?
>
> Athletes also set high realistic goals for themselves and train and play hard.
>
> What high realistic goals have you set for yourself?

Athletes are successful because they are pursuing their goals and enjoying their sport. Their sport enriches their lives and they believe that what they get back is worth what they put into their sport. If you play sport or have young people who play sport – what do you get out of it?

Jack J. Lesyk from the Ohio Center for Sport Psychology (Sportpsych.org, 2018)[3] also suggests nine specific skills that contribute to success and can be found here. The interesting point is that these skills are not specific to sport. These same mental skills are in fact transferable into other areas of life and can be improved with instruction and practice whatever age you are.

These nine skills are:

1. Choose and maintain a positive attitude.
2. Maintain a high level of self-motivation.
3. Set high, realistic goals.
4. Deal effectively with people.
5. Use positive self-talk.
6. Use positive mental imagery.
7. Manage anxiety effectively.
8. Manage emotions effectively.
9. Maintain concentration.

Let's look at each of the nine skills.

Choose and maintain a positive attitude

I guess by now you're probably getting the idea that if you want to be more successful you need to realize that your attitude is a choice, so work towards an attitude that is predominantly positive. Also view working through this book as an opportunity to compete against yourself. Learn from the successes you experience whilst trying new things out.

Work towards pursuing excellence, not perfection, and realize that you and everyone else in the world are not perfect. Try to maintain balance and perspective between your passion and the rest of your life. Finally, respect yourself and everyone you encounter.

EXERCISE 19:
Do you have a positive attitude?

Rate your ability to have a positive attitude below.
1 = negative, 10 = positive.

Negative				Neutral		Positive			
1	2	3	4	5	6	7	8	9	10

If you didn't score yourself a 10 what do you need to do to make a 10?

Maintain a high level of self-motivation

Let's assume for the moment that you have the right ATTITUDE now. The next step is to be aware of the rewards and benefits you stand to get if you are motivated enough to follow through on your vision. However, you will need to be resilient and persist through difficult tasks and difficult times. This is even more important when these rewards and benefits are not immediately forthcoming.

EXERCISE 20:
How motivated are you?

___

How motivated are you on a scale of 1 to 10? Circle which one applies to you right now.

Low				Neutral		High			
1	2	3	4	5	6	7	8	9	10

If you didn't score yourself a 10 what do you need to do to make it a 10?

___

___

___

Set high, realistic goals

Athletes wouldn't perform as well as they do without setting themselves some SMART goals which can be short, medium and long-term goals or a combination. The acronym SMART means Specific, Measurable, Achievable, Realistic and Timely.

An example would be:

SPECIFIC – To spend quality time with my kids with no interruptions

MEASURABLE – 1 hour a day

ACHIEVABLE – Yes, because if you'd said 37 hours and had a full-time job this goal might not be achievable

REALISTIC – For most people this would be a realistic goal

TIMELY OR TIME BOUND – Every day from 6-7pm or whatever fits your schedule

To begin with you need to understand your current performance levels. For example, how much uninterrupted time do you spend with your kids now?

I recently met a CEO of a large multinational at a conference in London who inadvertently overheard a conversation between his son and his friend at home one evening.

His son's friend said, "I'm really looking forward to the weekend. My dad and I always do something together; it's great. What are you doing with your dad?" The CEO's son replied, "Nothing, he's always at work!" That really stunned and upset the father and motivated him to rethink his relationships at home. Now father and son have what they both say is an excellent relationship based on better quality time together.

Please now set a SMART goal for yourself. This should include the young people in your household. The example given above is a great way to bring the family together to discuss and plan what the future could look like. Your SMART goal may equally be something completely different.

An example might be: my short-term goal is to spend one day a month with my family from DD/MM/YYYY.

EXERCISE 21:
My goals

_____

My short-term 1-year SMART goal is _____

My medium-term 2-3-year SMART goal is _____

My long-term 4-5-year SMART goal is _____

How committed are you on a scale of 1 to 100? If you're not committed 100% then don't set goals that you are never going to achieve.

Deal effectively with people

Successful people know that they are part of a larger system that includes partners, family, friends, co-workers, and other people in their life. Communication often breaks down when we do not communicate our thoughts and feeling to the people we should be talking to. We also need to listen to other people's views without responding; just listen.

Many successful people have already learnt the skills and capabilities needed for dealing with conflict, difficult people and other people when they are negative or oppositional.

A great example here comes from my experiences working with students and employees in businesses. There was a CEO with a big personality and a forceful way of getting his message across. His managers felt overwhelmed and negative about their work because they felt they weren't being listened to, just dictated to. Two managers wanted to resign at this point.

I held a mediation meeting for the group. In the meeting everyone had the opportunity to say what they felt was wrong. They also had to come up with a suggestion as to how to move forward. They then started working together as a team and continually worked on their communication skills.

EXERCISE 22:
Improving your communication skills

Reflect on your own people skills. Write down one thing that you could work on to improve your people skills.

Use positive self-talk

Life often throws us curveballs to deal with, and often several of them at a time. How you deal with each event is important. Successful people maintain their self-confidence during these difficult events by talking to themselves with realistic, positive self-talk.

Imagining that you're talking through a difficult time with your best friend, talk to yourself and ask, "What would my best friend say to me right now?"

Self-talk should be used to regulate your thoughts, feelings and behaviours each day and especially during difficult times.

EXERCISE 23:
Difficult situations

Think of a difficult situation either now or recently. How did you react? How could you, or did you, maintain your self-confidence?

_____

_____

_____

_____

Use positive mental imagery

There are a vast number of different techniques you could use and please do feel free to explore different types of mental imagery so that you find one that works best for you.

For example, guided imagery harnesses the brain's natural tendency to create vivid mental representations of our beliefs, desires, experiences and goals. You can create positive mental imagery by yourself by sitting or lying in a warm comfortable place and relaxing. You can then create and use mental images that are detailed, specific and realistic. For example, if you're a footballer – you could practise hearing the roar of the crowd as the ball goes in the net.

You can also download audio guides which will help you to take part in imagery because both athletes and successful people prepare themselves for challenging situations by imagining themselves performing well.

Psychologists' research suggests that imagery is effective for a variety of issues including stress and anxiety and helps athletes perform. Tiger Woods the golfer has been frank about his use of imagery to improve his game. Other famous people who use imaging include Jim Carrey, Arnold Schwarzenegger, Oprah Winfrey, Wayne Rooney, Jonny Wilkinson and Andy Murray – they all use visualization to do their best work.

I've also used mental imagery techniques with a coach. I remember sitting in a chair with my eyes closed and my coach asked me to watch a film of myself at a point in the future. This worked for me because I'm a visual learner. The trick is to write or draw what you saw during the visualization so that you remember where you want to get to in the future.

EXERCISE 24:
Mental wellbeing

What tools and techniques will you explore to improve your positive mental wellbeing?

Manage anxiety effectively

Almost all of us will have anxiety in our lives at one time or another. Some forms of anxiety are good in that they can help you to perform well. The trick is to know when anxiety is taking over your life and know how and when to reduce it.

I'll share with you the types of anxiety that I encounter from time to time. I often don't know when I'm getting anxious. There are triggers that I sometimes ignore which include: being more serious, loss of humour, working all hours, feeling faint, stomach cramps, lack of concentration, and getting quietly annoyed with people but not understanding why. When I'm anxious I also don't like to be around lots of people, preferring to be on my own. I also worry about things that haven't happened yet.

The symptoms of anxiety for all of us can start out the same – as just feeling generally anxious – but get worse or last longer than they should. These include:

- Feeling frightened, nervous or panicky all the time
- Getting down or depressed
- Difficulty sleeping
- Low appetite
- Lack of concentration
- Tired and irritable
- Palpitations – when your heart feels like it's racing
- Dry mouth
- Trembling
- Feeling faint
- Stomach cramps and/or diarrhoea

Feeling one, some or even most of the above doesn't necessarily mean you have anxiety. It's important to talk to your GP to get a full diagnosis. For today, as you read this book, do any of these symptoms resonate with you? Which ones?

_____

_____

_____

_____

Manage your emotions effectively

A positive and successful person accepts emotions such as excitement, anger, and disappointment as part of their life's rich experience. Instead of reacting negatively they can use these emotions to improve their reactions to difficult situations, rather than let the emotions interfere with their lives.

I travel a lot and hear many different people talking to one another or communicating with each other on their mobile phones. You only have to listen in to these conversations to know that they are not able to manage their emotions effectively.

When something goes wrong, doesn't work out, or they can't get what they want, the volume of their voice starts to rise. Additionally, shouting and being aggressive soon follows and then the use of the F word to add colour and flavour to the conversation.

I've experienced this firsthand with university students in the early stages of their studies. Even last week I had to call a mediation meeting to chat about the group's lack of ability to communicate with each other. There are possibly many reasons for this inability to communicate, including the use of mobile devices which we often see in restaurants where everyone at the table is 'together' but not really because everyone is on a mobile device. You might think that this section of the book is written with just young people in mind but it's not. Stop for a moment and consider your own behaviour and communication – what could you do more of, less of, or differently?

Maintain concentration

Successful people know what they must pay attention to in any given situation. It's important for them to maintain focus and resist all distractions, whether they come from the outside environment or from within themselves. On the occasions that successful people lose concentration they can regain their focus quickly. They live in the here-and-now without regard to either the past or future events.

EXERCISE 25:
Maintaining concentration

Reflect on the last few months – can you think of an example when you found it difficult to maintain concentration? What were you thinking about instead? What could you do differently?

_____

_____

_____

_____

_____

_____

I've covered a lot of ground in this chapter, so let's pull it all together now.

EXERCISE 26:
Mental skills

Choose one of the nine mental skills above to work on this month

I have chosen to work on the mental skill of

_____

this month because _____

_____

_____

(i) FACT

I want to give you an example of someone I met recently who experienced a negative image of herself. We along with 20 other people were attending the Business Empires event in London. As part of that event we were invited to a day-long coaching session with Mike Koenig from the USA.

During our coaching session the group were discussing the title and content of our books. One young lady explained that her book was about the "undocumented citizens of the world". If you're not sure what the terms mean, the easy definition of an undocumented immigrant is that he or she is a foreign-born person who doesn't have a legal right to be or remain in the United States, in this individual case. However, the situation is much more complicated than this simple definition.

She explained that she was writing a book about her life story and told everyone in the group that she didn't know why anyone would want to listen to her or read her book. The rest of the room gasped with horror and responded, "Have you not thought about being a thought leader in your field of experience and telling your story to the world?" At that point she became emotionally overwhelmed as did we all.

She hadn't considered herself worthy enough to finish the book and get it published. As a group we collectively encouraged her to continue with the book because the world needs to know about her message and what she's been through in her life to date. To be a stateless person must be a really difficult thing to live with; she had been deported from the USA.

After the coaching had finished her body language and negative mental image of herself changed within minutes. She chose to maintain a positive attitude and become a positive role model for all the displaced people in the world. That was a very magical moment for the rest of us in the group.

She became self-motivated to finish her book and set herself high realistic goals to publish it this year. Using positive mental imagery, she now wants to become the voice of displaced people in the world and to help these people move forward with their lives. This lady has already shown many of the nine mental skills needed to be successful and is working on the others to fulfil her dreams.

Yet it took a group of complete strangers to inspire and support her to continue with her book. So, my message is that you're not on your own; there are people out there waiting to help you. This young lady also had other challenges in her life but writing the book was a kind of therapy for her. Of all the challenges she was facing she chose to focus on finishing her book instead of trying to solve everything in one go.

⚠ WARNING:

Big warning here! This is a problem that I run into with many people that I coach. What happens is that people take on too many challenges in one go and try to achieve multiple goals at the same time. In some cases, people completely give up on the hard work they've done so far which doesn't have the positive effect they want to achieve. I want you to be aware of this and think "If I could only solve one challenge, which is the most important to me, and would make me a happier person?"

The key is to then break down your goals into bite-sized pieces. How do you do this? You could choose to coach yourself although you wouldn't get an independent viewpoint and anyone challenging your assumptions. Or you may decide to work with a coach, which is what I'm going to discuss in the next chapter.

CHAPTER 7

Life Overload: How to Make It Through the Day with a Coach

This chapter is about what a coach is, how a coach can help you and how to find the right coach. The ideas here will help parents, carers, those over 18 and career advisers to find and work with a coach.

It's OK to ask for help; I did. So, what if you need inspiration and support from a coach? It is personal. So, I've done some research amongst the best coaches in the world and asked them what the process is for choosing a coach. Here's some premium advice from them.

What is a coach?

A professional coach is someone who will help you identify and focus on what's important, which in turn accelerates your success. A great coach will also create a safe environment in which you can see yourself more clearly and will also identify gaps between where you are right now and where you want to get to.

A coach can also help you get from point A to point B faster than you could on your own, because fear often holds people back and a coach will support you to overcome fear and make those important decisions and actions which help you to move forward.

A coach will also ask you to reflect upon your thoughts, actions and behaviours and will ask the uncomfortable questions you probably wouldn't deal with yourself and give you the support you need to make the changes you want. They will also guide and support you by holding you accountable to ensure that there is a sustained commitment which leads to change.

There are many different types of coaching available and in the next section I'm going to explain the types of coaching we use as Jack Canfield coaches with a system that has achieved proven results for over 40 years.

How a coach can help you

The diagram below shows you the more general areas where a coach could help you.

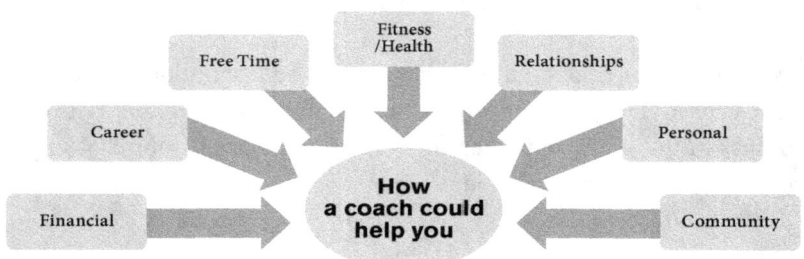

Finance coaching

There's an old saying that "Money can't buy happiness." I don't think it does, but that said, most people will agree that money does help towards it to some extent. This is because money can reduce the stresses and pressures of life because it enables people to pay bills and put food on the table. However, those who struggle financially often find themselves in extremely stressful situations.

A coach will work with you to look at your income and expenditure. Jack Canfield coaches will normally start from where you are now financially, and work with you to find your ideal situation in your mind's eye. As I said before, accepting 100% responsibility for where you are now is the first step to getting more money into your life. Instead of burying your head in the sand, a coach will encourage you to face the issues head-on so that you can make the changes you want in your life. Sometimes the problem lies in behaviours and habits that have built up over many years and may take time to change.

Unless your coach is also a financial adviser they will not give you financial advice, but they will be able to point you in the direction of organizations that can support you. Assess your finances using the exercises in Chapter 8.

Career and business coaching

Whether you are a business owner, an executive, a manager, an employee or simply a person looking for a new job or career, working with a business or career coach to help develop and hone your skills could greatly improve your chances of success.

Business owners already know that coaching has an impact on an organization's financial performance; according to an International Coach Federation and Human Capital Institute study, 60% of respondents from organizations with strong coaching cultures report their revenue to be above average, compared to their peer group.

When it comes to building your personal brand as an executive, employee or if you are looking for a job, a coach can be a powerful resource who can help you get out of your own way, stand out, and take action to achieve the things that are truly important to you.

A coach can help you to:

- Get clear about your goals and help you stay focused
- Gain an external, objective and constructive perspective of your situation

A coach will also help you to identify blind spots and work with you to identify potential career opportunities that maybe you hadn't thought of before. Jack Canfield coaches help you to identify your core values and help you to create the career path you really want to follow as well as helping you to cut through the clutter of what's currently holding you back.

You may even be able to get your company to foot the bill. Talk to your manager and/or your talent development staff. They might be willing to invest in coaching for you if you make a good case for it. Also, some leadership development programmes come with coaching components so sign up for those if you can. It's a great way to experience coaching. And if your company chooses not to pay for your coaching, make the investment yourself. It will pay off in clarity, happiness and increased success. Think of coaching as an investment, not an expense.

The term 'business coaching' encompasses:

- Executive coaching (for middle and senior managers)
- Start-up business coaching (for entrepreneurs)
- Management coaching (for team leaders)
- Staff coaching (for teams)
- Interview coaching (for potential employees)
- Career coaching
- Leadership coaching

Coaching to get more free time in your life

Let's focus for a moment on your free time; that's if you have any! Most of us spend most of our time at work but what's the point of life if you have no free time to do things that are fun and that you enjoy doing?

We all give reasons and excuses for why we can't find the time for ourselves and many of you will sometimes feel frustrated that everything and everyone has priority over what you want to do. A coach will support and guide you towards getting more free time in your life which will ultimately help you to live a more balanced lifestyle.

There is an exercise in Chapter 8 which will help you to identify whether you have enough free time in your life. If the answers to the questions are next to zero it's probably time to rethink this area of your life.

If you had more free time what would you be doing with your family and friends? What hobbies would you like to pursue? What kinds of holidays would you like to take? What would you do for fun? How could you meet new people? What new thing could you try in your life?

Fitness and health coaching

Many of us want to be fit and healthy, but what does a healthy life mean? In general, it refers to the choices we make to improve and support our health and fitness. The wellness industry is now huge in the West and therefore it's much easier to find information about fitness and health. However, there is so much different conflicting advice out there so why not work with a professional health coach? A coach can guide you through the changes you want to make.

Healthy living is about making choices and decisions daily. Over time we often develop unhealthy habits and behaviours. For example, one glass of wine turns into two, and then three, and we excuse ourselves because we're under stress or something similar. It can take years to develop unhealthy habits and behaviours and weeks or months to accept that change needs to happen.

Other examples you might be familiar with include:

- Joining a gym and never going
- An unbalanced diet
- A lack of sleep
- Not drinking plenty of water
- Working long hours without a break
- Feeling stressed much of the time
- Poor work/life balance

The point is that nothing will change until you decide you want to change the situation you find yourself in, and work with a coach who will support you to achieve your goals and aspirations.

Relationship coaching

Work isn't everything although I have been guilty of thinking that it was during my lifetime! Some of the most important relationships we make in life are not at work but usually lie with family and friends. Relationships are sometimes tested during difficult situations and a coach can help you to:

- Resolve relationship difficulties between partners
- Work on resolving a work/life balance for the family
- Bring up the young people in your life to follow their own passions
- Work out how to help and support teenagers
- Help deal with life after separation or divorce
- Help people work through redundancy or severance

Jack Canfield coaches provide people with the tools and techniques to resolve conflicts, reach compromises and even transform a difficult situation into a better one for everyone involved. Try out the exercise in Chapter 8 to assess which of your relationships could do with improving.

Personal goals coaching

The aim of a personal development coach is to help you to evaluate and assess your current strengths and weaknesses, opportunities and threats. The principles of coaching are similar to the way coaches work with athletes. There isn't much difference between world-class athletes, celebrities and the rest of us. Believe it or not, they still experience the same challenges and emotions you and I go through daily.

Let's think about that for a moment. One of the differences between being a world-class athlete and the rest of us is that you'd never expect an athlete to reach the Olympic Games without a world-class coach. Successful athletes obviously understand the power of coaching because coaches help athletes to help them to achieve their goals far more effectively than if they trained alone.

Let's take another sporting analogy. You generally wouldn't expect a professional football team to enter the stadium without a whole team of coaches. Well, today, coaching has moved into the business and personal realm to include coaches who have succeeded in your area of interest – and who can help you traverse this same path or even one far greater. You too can be world class, whatever that looks like and feels like to you.

Let's take another example of those with celebrity status. They too can feel fear and can get overwhelmed. It's also no secret that celebrities can have issues with money, substance abuse, health, feelings of self-worth and relationships. Mainly because they're human just like me and you.

The use of a life coach has helped many celebrities work through roadblocks they encounter to take their lives to the next level. Other than their notoriety, celebrities are no different from anyone else. Just because they can be easily recognized on the streets doesn't mean they're not fighting an internal battle.

Oprah Winfrey has attributed some of her success to her personal life coach, Martha Beck. She has been a major advocate for life coaching as a result. Over the last 25 years, she's presented a multitude of life coaches to her fans and strongly suggests her viewers use a life coach to succeed.

Leonardo DiCaprio has worked with the head honcho of life coaching, Tony Robbins. Maybe it was Tony's idea for Leo to stand in a freezing river while eating raw fish during the filming of *The Revenant*. DiCaprio is quiet about his experiences with Robbins, but his success and persistence speak for themselves. Even though he fell short on numerous Oscar wins for Best Actor, DiCaprio quietly continued to master his craft and focus on doing the job. He was finally able to take home the shiny gold statue after winning the Best Actor award in *The Revenant*. Good for you, Leo. It was long overdue.

During her career, one of the Williams sisters (Serena) was constantly battling injuries to stay on the court. As you can imagine, the constant gruel of playing through injuries can take its toll when you're a high-performing athlete. She worked with – you guessed it – Tony Robbins to persist and train through her injuries. It paid off in the end because she won a Grand Slam of the Australian Open in 2009. No big deal.

Now, I'm not suggesting for a moment that you want to attain celebrity status or be at the Olympic Games (but you might want to). However, if you want to make changes in your life then working with a coach often speeds up the process for you and gives you a different perspective on the challenges you're facing. A coach will also help you to achieve your goals because they will hold you accountable throughout the coaching process.

Once you've decided to move forward a coach will explore with you your ideas which may include you considering going back to education and studying again, getting some training, or attending a workshop. Or, perhaps, seeking therapy for a past hurt, divorce, redundancy or emotional trauma, taking up a hobby e.g. learning to play an instrument, starting a new sport or art class, taking up running or writing a book. If you love to travel, talk about all the places you'd like to visit. These ideas are not an exhaustive list but are here to trigger a discussion with a coach.

Community coaching

Finally, let's focus on the community you live in. I often coach people to be more involved with their local and global communities. This is because many of us have lost touch with the communities in which we live for a number of reasons. However, working in the community has several benefits including:

- Developing skills
- Making contacts
- Improving the quality of life for others
- Exploring your personal strengths and weaknesses
- Developing employability skills
- Feeling happier in yourself
- Reductions in stress levels

As part of leading a successful, healthy balanced lifestyle a Jack Canfield coach will encourage you to check out all the different kinds of community activities that take place in your area and ask you how could you become a valued member of your community. How could you make a difference in your local community? Who could you help? Engaging with the local community is a great way for both adults and young people to make a difference. For young people volunteering in the community is a great way to build up their employability skills and capabilities. Adding them to a CV tells potential employers that you are not just qualified but have continued with some personal development.

Qualifications are great, but employers are more likely to interview a candidate if they have something else about them. This is an important point to make to undergraduate students because a degree on its own no longer guarantees them a job. I spend a lot of time visiting universities encouraging undergraduates to get work experience or volunteer or join a club to enhance their skills and capabilities before they graduate.

Many of the young people I have worked with have volunteered to do all sorts of work in their communities, and in some cases this has led to permanent jobs. Certainly the experience is of great value to anyone, and the community in which they live.

If you are out of a job at the moment, being part of the community will help your self-confidence and self-esteem and may lead to opportunities you never thought possible. This happened to me and I continue to get great pleasure out of my voluntary work with the Careers and Enterprise Company and with the Education Business Partnership South (EBP).

How to choose the right coach for you

Choose someone you can get on with; start by talking to any prospective coach for 15 minutes to gauge your chemistry. Check in with how you feel right after the talk. A good sign is if you feel excited and inspired by your discussion, but a bit scared. This typically means that you're inspired to grow, ready to commit to the process, but part of you is 'scared' because you know there will be some stretching involved. That's a good sign, indicating the coach will facilitate moving you beyond your comfort zone (which is essential if you want growth).

Find a coach who's done what you want to do in the world. Don't buy into that myth that the coach doesn't have to know a thing about what you're trying to do. If you want to make a million dollars in your new business, for instance, don't go to a 'life coach'; go to a coach who possesses deep entrepreneurial experience, has lived what you're trying to do, and has had great success. If you want to transform your career, go to someone who has reinvented theirs successfully and has helped hundreds of others do the same.

Also, check out their thought leadership (what are they recognised for in their field of expertise?). What does it say about them? Do you love their website, their LinkedIn profile, their articles, their guest posts, and other components of thought leadership? After watching their videos and reading their material, you should feel like you simply can't wait to work with them.

Get a sense of their 'energy'. Every coach, and every person on this planet, has a certain style, approach, worldview and energy to their work. Make sure it's a good fit with your style. Decide what you are up for! Do you want your coach to understand you or do you want him or her to shake up your thinking? The answer to this question has implications for the type of relationship you are seeking from your coach.

If you choose a coach with a similar background to yours, who may have faced the same challenges as you in a similar context, then they are well equipped to support your thinking from that experience. This could take the form of them challenging you to think through specific aspects of your role and probing your ways of dealing with scenarios that are familiar to them.

A coach with a more challenging style will likely unsettle you and force you to confront a few things. Both types of coaching relationships can be extremely helpful, and which one you choose to engage has a lot to do with what is currently going on in your life and the existing supports (or lack thereof) that you have.

Decide if you want your coach to be someone who has the same experience (in the same role or industry) as you or is outside the field in which you are working. Unlike corporate consulting, coaching is 'content free', not a place for the coach to provide you with detailed business advice and opinions, so this is an interesting decision to make.

Identifying the right coach is not about simply finding a good fit. There are many people we like or feel a fit with. Getting a friendly vibe from a coach won't necessarily correlate with tangible impact on your professional growth. Instead, look for 'fit for purpose'. Ask yourself: can this coach help me achieve my personal and/or professional growth objectives in an enjoyable way? More specifically, to figure out if they're 'fit for purpose', in your introductory meeting with a coach, seek answers to these questions:

- Does the coach exude a brand of professionalism that I respect and a style that I'm comfortable with?

- Is the coach capturing both my strengths and opportunities with his/her questions?
- Can the coach articulate his/her model of coaching and examples of how he/she has helped other executives thrive professionally?

If what you observe and hear resonates with both your heart and your mind, then you've found your ideal coach.

These suggestions offer a variety of time-tested perspectives. I have had a lot of experience working with coaches, both through working with the Jack Canfield group of trainers and through my own experience when working with clients. I strongly believe that finding the right coach is an invaluable way to get clear about your goals, achieve success, and increase the joy in your life.

TIP:

If there are a great number of coaches to review, go with your first instinct or gut reaction.

WARNING:

Coaching can seriously improve your life! You cannot, under any circumstances, work with a coach and expect that nothing will change. This is because by the time you've decided to hire a coach you really want something in your life to change. This is vital!

And... because you purchased this book, the chances are you are interested in an aspect of coaching to improve your life, or that of the young people in your life. In the early stages why not have a free, no obligation talk with me by visiting http://bit.ly/LKStrachan. This website gives you the opportunity to see how I could help you, your business and the young people in your life. Here you can also book some time out for a chat about the future. Note, while it's free, I'm always busy, and availability may be limited, but it's a great opportunity to get your online chat booked with me.

Since you are reading and implementing the principles and practices in this book I thought I'd also give away an extra bonus so I'm offering you a free e-book called *Living the Success Principles* to say thank you for working towards a better life for you and the young people in your life. I hope you enjoy reading it. The book can be accessed here: http://bit.ly/Free-e-b

CHAPTER 8

Reflecting on Where You Are Now

The previous chapter explained what a coach is, how a coach can help you and how you can go about finding the right coach. To help you think about the changes you want to make, now would be a great time to assess where you are at this moment.

EXERCISE 27
Assessing your finances

Finance coaching

If you want to control your outgoings, or are in debt, write down your answers to these questions:

1. Where could you cut your spending – even by a small amount?

_____

2. How could you increase your income?

_____

Writing things down can really help you to face the fear of doing something about them. Your money worries will start to melt away just by getting your fears out of your mind and down on paper. So, what's your plan of action?

_____

_____

_____

_____

_____

Example: I go to a lot of dance classes and often pay in advance for a 10-week course for a reduced rate. As I travel and work away a lot I never manage to get to all 10 classes. So I was giving money away and even though I had got a discount for buying 10 lessons it was still costing me more money, so I stopped paying in advance and pay as I go now. It's a small step to take but could save you money if you decided to do something similar. How much is that gym membership costing you right now?

EXERCISE 28:
What type of career coaching do you need?

Career and business coaching

Write down the areas where you feel coaching would help you achieve your goals and increase your success in the box below.

_____

_____

_____

_____

_____

_____

_____

_____

_____

_____

EXERCISE 29:
Free time

Coaching to get more free time in your life

Let's focus for a moment on your free time; that's if you have any! Most of us spend most of our time at work but what's the point of life if you have no free time to do things that are fun and that you enjoy doing?

A few questions will help you to identify whether you have enough free time in your life.

1. What are you doing with your family?

_____

2. What are you doing with your friends?

_____

3. What would you if you had more free time in your life?

_____

4. What does having free time mean to you?

_____

5. When was the last time you tried something new?

_____

6. What kinds of holiday do you take?

_____

7. What do you do for fun?

_____

If the answers to the questions are next to zero it's probably time to rethink this area of your life. If you had more free time what would you be doing with your family and friends? What hobbies would you like to pursue? What kinds of holidays would you like to take? What would you do for fun? How could you meet new people? What new thing could you try in your life?

EXERCISE 30:
Fitness and health coaching

_____

Fitness and health coaching

A few questions will help you to identify whether you are fit and healthy.

1. Are you free of all disease?

_____

2. Are you pain-free?

_____

3. How long do you plan to live for?

_____

4. Are you open and relaxed all day long?

_____

5. Are you full of vitality?

_____

6. Are you flexible as well as strong?

_____

7. Do you exercise, eat good food, and drink lots of water?

_____

8. How much do you weigh?

_____

EXERCISE 31:
Relationship coaching

Relationship coaching

What type of relationship coaching do you need?

Write down the areas where you feel relationship coaching would help you achieve you goals and increase your success in the box below.

_____

_____

_____

_____

_____

_____

_____

_____

_____

_____

EXERCISE 32:
Personal development coaching

To find out whether life coaching is for you, think about the questions and write your answers in the right-hand column:

	Yes/No	Why?
Would you like to improve your communication skills?		
What would it feel like to be more confident?		
Do you want to improve your self-esteem?		
Do you want to be more passionate, and motivated about what you do?		
Do you want or need to learn more skills to advance further in life?		
Would you like to feel happier with your whole life?		
Are you ready to take 100% responsibility and implement your action plan?		

EXERCISE 33:
Community coaching

What are your plans to explore and learn about and take part in your local or global community initiatives?

CHAPTER 9

Follow-up Framework

First off, I have provided you with example exercises throughout the book and these can also be found on my website, where all the exercises are in Word format so that you can download them and easily use them. They can be found here: http://bit.ly/Free4Members. You'll need to join as a member to access the resources but there are no membership fees – enjoy.

Just the facts

- Coaching is important, but it's equally important that you take 100% responsibility for moving your own life forward. No-one should be reading this book and taking no action at all because what would be the point?
- Don't just read this book, implement – implement – implement!
- It's important to keep regular contact with your coach: fire off an email or phone call once a month to keep in contact with your coach and keep yourself at the top of their minds.
- Keep going because as Lao Tzu once said:

    "A journey of a thousand miles begins with a single step."

CHAPTER 10

Where Do I Go from Here?

In typical circumstances, once you've read a self-help guide like this, it's likely you'll want to read more books. So I'm recommending some further reading here that I've read myself and found helpful. They're usually available in print and/or electronically, and if you're worried about the expenses, think about buying a second-hand book or get your local library to order it in for you.

All the books listed are suitable for young adults and adults who'd prefer to be young adults again, so enjoy!

- *Getting There: A Book of Mentors* by Gillian Zoe Segal

- *How to Stop Worrying and Start Living* by Dale Carnegie

- *How to Win Friends and Influence People* by Dale Carnegie

- *Learned Optimism* by Martin Seligman

- *The Magic of Thinking Big* by David J. Schwartz

- *The Power of Now* by Eckhart Tolle

- *The Power of Positive Thinking* by Norman Vincent Peale
- *The Road Less Travelled* by M. Scott Peck
- *The 4-hour Work Week* by Timothy Ferriss
- *The 7 Habits of Highly Effective People* by Stephen R. Covey
- *The Happiness Project* by Gretchen Rubin
- *The Success Principles* by Jack Canfield
- *The Tao of Pooh* by Benjamin Hoff
- *Unlimited Power* by Anthony Robbins
- *Think and Grow Rich!* by Napoleon Hill
- *You Can Heal Your Life* by Louise Hay

There are an almost unlimited number of books you can track down, so if a topic you want isn't listed here, go online or into a bookshop, have a coffee and browse the shelves.

CHAPTER 11

How to Get Help

How to find people to help you

First, by now you'll agree that we're probably in a time-sensitive world with urgent issues on your calendar right now. It may not seem like it now, but when you look back on this book 6-18 months from now, you'll be happy that you've changed your life and have more time to do what you want and you'll wish you'd done it sooner.

The door to achieving the life you want for you and your young people is WIDE open right now, but it will close fast if you do not implement the tools and techniques in this book… and I would not want you to miss out on securing the future you want.

In the interest of full disclosure, we provide a turnkey, 100% service which means that you can work with us on any aspect of your life. Plus, we know how to get results faster than anyone. Our services are expensive, and you will probably be able to find someone to do a bare-bones job for much less. But the way to look at it is: we invest a lot of money into our clients' future. And when you get the results you want, we all win.

But we're restricting ourselves to only a handful of clients at a time and while that's not to say we won't take you, there's a good chance we will be committed already and may have to pass.

Having said all of that, if you feel that we could work together, and you'd like to find out about my team's availability to help you and to get all of this DONE, please contact me at:

Phone: #44 (0)7739 172447
Email: lesley@lesleystrachan.co.uk
Web: https://lesley-strachan-consulting-training.com/

I will, at the very least, be able to tell you if we have availability to work with you.

If we decide to move forward with you, we always start with a diagnosis. There is no obligation on either your or our part. This just begins the discussion as to how we may be able to help you. And while we know that some people will rightly explore several coaching services and then go and hire a cheap service, we also know that the best customers, those who understand the value of getting themselves from where they are to where they want to be, will just say "Let's work together." We are looking for a small number of clients to work with and if that sounds like you, then please feel free to write or call.

With that, I bid you adieu. You've reached the end of this book, but you certainly haven't reached the end of how we can help you. If you've followed all the techniques and processes in this book and really took it to heart, you're very prepared to wade into your new life and come out the victor; you're ahead of most of the population and you have a clear idea of what lies in store. Don't get complacent, be creative, and you'll be successful in forging the life you want for you, and your young people, for many years to come!

BIBLIOGRAPHY

1. Dr. Deirdre Hughes. 2018. We are letting Britain's young people down. [Online] Available at: https://www.fenews.co.uk/featured-article/14654-we-are-letting-britain-s-young-people-down. [Accessed 9 March 2018]

2. Steve Taylor Ph.D. 2018. The Power of Purpose. [Online] Available at: https://www.psychologytoday.com/blog/out-the-darkness/201307/the-power-purpose. [Accessed 9 March 2018]

3. Sportpsych.org. (2018). Ohio Center for Sport Psychology. [Online] Available at: https://www.sportpsych.org/nine-mental-skills-overview [Accessed 5 March 2018]

ABOUT THE AUTHOR

I am an executive education and coaching company and I free you up from the day-to-day stuff, so you can learn, grow and develop you and/or your business.

I'm about helping you to move past the constraints you've created so that you can focus on what's more important to you.

I'm about freedom of choice – 'freedom to learn, grow and develop'.

My purpose is to use my creativity and experience to support and inspire people through education and coaching all over the world and have fun doing it.

As a certified Jack Canfield trainer in the Success Principles all our programmes are delivered in the UK, Europe, USA and Australia in English in the education and corporate sectors.

Our team works with people based upon 8 core values: continuous learning – an entrepreneurial mindset – coaching for success – creative advice – independence – courage – leadership and a positive approach.

I have owned several micro and small businesses as well as working for corporate organizations as a marketing practitioner and trainer.

I hold an MBA, am a Master SimVenture (http://simventure.co.uk) trainer for business simulation games and hold a postgraduate certificate in research methods. Further qualifications include: Diploma in Management, Senior Fellow of The Higher Education Academy, Member of The Chartered Institute of Marketing (http://www.cim.co.uk), The Institute of Small Business and Entrepreneurship (http://isbe.org.uk) and The Association of Learning Technologists (https://www.alt.ac.uk). I am an active researcher and my work has been published extensively in academic journals and conference presentations. I am also a mentor for The Education and Business Partnership (https://www.ebpsouth.co.uk) in the UK and a Schools Enterprise Adviser for The Careers and Enterprise Company (https://www.careersandenterprise.co.uk).

As I work with many young people I also hold a certificate from the Disclosure and Barring Service (DBS) Registration code: C7307749351 so that parents can be assured the correct background checks have been completed.

Helping you to face life changes

My programmes are based on 40 years of experience and are particularly powerful for people going through any kind of change in their lives, at home or at work, students at college or university, people wanting to get a job, or to get into the job market, and anyone facing challenges in their life, however big or small. My aim is to help individuals and businesses get from where they are to where they want to be using the timeless principles and practices used by the world's most successful men and women.

Areas of expertise include: coaching, communication, corporate training, education, health and wellness, leadership, personal coaching, personal growth and development, workshops, sales, marketing, young adults and work-life balance.

How I can help you

I help people just like you to:

- Create space to have more time to think
- Rebuild lives during and after divorce, loss, retirement, 'empty nests', redundancy, injury or illness
- Overcome procrastination
- Make those important decisions to move on
- Let go of something that's bothering you or holding you back
- Be more assertive
- Manage difficult people and relationships – families, social life, and work
- Work through career changes whether voluntary or imposed

Book Lesley to speak at your next event

Would you like me to speak or hold a workshop at your next event?

Our programmes are designed to be optimal for a group of 10 or more. We can focus your event on specific areas of personal development so that you get the most out of the time we spend together. To find out more about what services we focus on please go to http://bit.ly/LesleyCoaching. Our team who perform this educational session have a combined experience of over 1,000 presentations. We have spoken at many events which you can check out here http://bit.ly/LesleySpeak.

Our programmes

We offer several different programmes including:

- Breaking Through Personal Barriers to Success
- Taking 100% Responsibility
- How to Get What You Want in Life
- Creativity, Innovation and Change
- Managing Change
- Careers and Enterprise for Young People
- Coaching and Mentoring

This list changes from time to time. For a complete list of topics please contact me at lesley@lesleystrachan.co.uk.

Inquire about how you can book me to speak at your event!

Every year I volunteer to speak to a limited number of groups and associations at no cost to them. To inquire about having me speak at your event for no charge contact me at lesley@lesleystrachan.co.uk.

Quantity Discounts

My books are found at the following booksellers.

- Amazon
- Waterstones
- Barnes & Noble
- Chapters/Indigo
- All major online bookstores

If you would like to offer this book at your next event or association meeting, I offer quantity discounts. For more information please contact lesley@lesleystrachan.co.uk

BONUS!

Discover exactly how you can make a few slight adjustments and begin to get from where you are to where you want to be… it all starts with YOU making some time to chat with me – http://bit.ly/LKStrachan.

If you want to chat, there is no obligation on either your or our part. This just begins the discussion as to how we may be able to help you.

Phone: 0044 (0) 7739 172447

Email: lesley@lesleystrachan.co.uk

www.ingramcontent.com/pod-product-compliance
Lightning Source LLC
Chambersburg PA
CBHW070147080526
44586CB00015B/1872